"The earth is a schoolroom for the soul's development. Our bodies are like the blue Tiffany box that holds a gift. Once the gift is removed, the box is discarded. The treasure remains."

—MARY T. BROWNE

By Mary T. Browne:

LOVE IN ACTION
LIFE AFTER DEATH: A Renowned Psychic Reveals
    What Happens to Us When We Die*

*Published by Ivy Books

LIFE AFTER DEATH

*A Renowned Psychic Reveals
What Happens to Us
When We Die*

Mary T. Browne

(formerly titled: *Mary T. Reflects
on the Other Side*)

IVY BOOKS • NEW YORK

Ivy Books
Published by Ballantine Books
Copyright © 1994 by Mary T. Browne

Library of Congress Catalog Card Number: 94-151

ISBN 0-8041-1386-6

Manufactured in the United States of America

First Hardcover Edition: May 1994
First Mass Market Edition: December 1995

10   9   8   7   6   5

*This book is dedicated
to the loving memory of*

*Sir William—an extraordinary teacher
George Wehner—a great psychic
Grace McQuillen—my grandmother
Katherine Carhart—my dear friend
Gloria Zimmerman—a great lady
Nicholas Callie—my friend who was like a brother to me
Robert F. Wood—my dear friend who was a truly great
lawyer*

*and to all our friends and
loved ones who have gone home.*

Contents

Acknowledgments

To my first editor, and dear friend, Julie Merberg, whose vision and support of this project made it possible.

To Virginia Faber, my editor, who asked all the right questions, and shared the vision.

My thanks to my agent, Jan Miller.

Marsha Losecar, for tirelessly typing the manuscript.

Joëlle Delbourgo, editor in chief, who since the beginning had faith in the book.

For the love and inspiration that flows to me from Margreta Overbeck and Ida MacGovern.

To Lawrence, for whom there are no sufficient words.

Introduction

I was born with a psychic gift. I had my first psychic experience when I was seven years old. At that age I saw the spirit of a woman who was so-called dead. This experience seemed perfectly normal and not at all frightening to me. I told my grandma Grace what I had witnessed. I was a bit surprised when she warned me not to talk about this event. She explained that people can be frightened of things they can't see. She went on to explain that I had a very special gift and that I'd been blessed.

Twelve years ago I began my professional psychic work. For years I had been giving informal readings for friends. Word of mouth brought me people who were seeking insights into their own lives. I had been pursuing a career as an actress and singer, but as the demand for my psychic gift grew, I left the theater.

Since then over five thousand individuals have come for private sessions. Whether it is a Wall Street broker, a typist, an Oscar-winning actor, a telephone operator, a student, or a psychiatrist, they have one thing in common: They're interested in a metaphysical point of view. And one of the most frequent topics of discussion among my clients is death—not in the morbid sense but from my metaphysical perspective.

We've heard different accounts of life after death from a variety of sources. Some people have had near-death experiences. Trance mediums, those gifted with the ability to channel messages from the departed, also relay information on the afterlife.

I've not had a personal near-death experience, nor do I consider myself a channel. My insights come from the sacred gifts of clairvoyance and clairaudience, which have enabled me to see departed souls and receive messages from them. I've seen clear pictures of the other side (the place we reside in once physical life ends) since early childhood. Messages from the other side have been given to me in different ways. Often I'm able to focus on an astral screen, using a form of psychic concentration that allows me to break through the barrier between earth and spirit. When I am looking at this screen, precise pictures of the spirit world and its inhabitants are shown to me. I am aided in this process by my spirit guide, White Feather. I've been visited by many of the spirits of the departed. I don't try to call anyone back to the earth. Those in spirit *choose* to visit me. I've also received messages from a number of people who've had near-death experiences. They have returned to physical life with communications for me from friends and teachers in spirit. These have been a great help and comfort to me.

I've done extensive work with the dying but more extensive work with the living. My life isn't spent in daily conversation with spirits, nor am I in a trance state, gazing for hours into the realms of the spirit world. The ability to see the other side is an important part of my work. But most of my time is spent concentrating on this life and the issues people have in the here and now.

We find the key to our happiness by understanding the continuity of life. We do not die, we pass over. We cast aside our physical bodies as we would cast aside an old garment. The spirit moves into the astral plane, the spirit world. The soul rests until the time it is ready to gather more experience. We are then reborn onto the earth, which is the schoolroom for the soul's development. We return to the earth until we have mastered ourselves. Each action that we perform affects not only this life but all lives to come. Everyone lives in the world, in the place he has earned by his own actions. This is true on earth and in the spirit world.

I choose to relate my experience with the afterlife in order to help you overcome the fear of death. And so that you may rejoice in the sacredness of this life.

The skeptic will have trouble understanding something that isn't physical or logical. He or she will wonder how I can be so certain there's an afterlife.

I can say only, *I know what I've seen.*

Do we question the doctor who diagnoses the patient as having poison ivy?

He knows what he's seen. Experience has taught him to recognize the look and feel of poison ivy. Experience has taught me to recognize the other side.

There's only a thin veil between the physical world and the spirit world, and the majority of mankind does not possess the psychic sense to see beyond the veil. I'm not the only person on earth with this ability. Throughout history there have been many gifted psychics and seers and there are many living today.

I can tell you only what I've seen and heard from the other world. I've pieced together this view of the afterlife from dozens of visions of the astral screen over the last thirty years, from accounts given me by my spirit guides and friends, from messages brought to me by people who survived near-death experiences. Based on what I've seen and learned, I hope to be able to paint a full picture of the other side for you. As you examine this picture, it will be apparent that this is a not a book about dying, but one about living, living on both sides of life.

✳ 1

Transition

The one inevitable fact in our lives is that we will die—or, as I prefer to say, "pass over" from the physical world to the spirit world, or astral plane. The transition from the physical realm to the spirit is not an ending; it is a transformation to another state of consciousness. Rather than limiting ourselves to thinking on a material physical level, we expand to fill an emotional, spiritual realm without bounds. Once we are freed from the physical body and are no longer consumed with the needs of the physical world, we can soar to new heights of learning.

Think about it! How many hours a day do we spend taking care of our bodies? We must feed them, wash them, make money to house them, clothe them, and so on. Sleep alone takes up a quarter of our earthly time. If we do not take proper care of our bodies, they start to break down. Illness then invades them and it can take a great deal of time and energy to repair the damage. The body is a divine machine, a machine so complex that mankind is still learning ways to keep it functioning properly.

Physical life can be described by the Sanskrit word *maya*, which means illusion. Hindu philosophy teaches that reality is all that is indestructible and eternal. Everything that is changeable and subject to decay and has a beginning and ending is perceived as *maya.* Since we know that each earth life is temporary, it follows that it is not real. It is *maya.* Simply, things are not always as they seem to be. A Chinese proverb warns us not to judge the house by its beautiful paint job. The external illusion leads us to believe that we will find a stable foundation. Experience teaches us that this is not true. Mistaking the façade for reality, we are in a state of *maya.* Believing that physical life is the only form of existence is an illusion. Thinking that we are dead once physical life ends is the ultimate illusion.

What Happens at the Time of Death

There are many written accounts of near-death experiences. What they have in common is that the people who have them come back to tell us of their adventure. They reach the border without a passport. Immigration sends them back home to get the proper documents.

During their short visit they are able to feel the vibrations of this new land. They can see many of the residents, smell new scents, and notice the different scenery. They become fascinated, then disappointed that they are not allowed to stay at that time.

Physical death (passing over) is our passport to a new land. Life in spirit is governed in a truly democratic manner. You arrive into the realm that you have earned through your own actions. The amount of money and connections you have in the physical world hold no power in this land. Your character is your position. The wisdom you have gained in your earthly incarnation can pave the road to bliss. It makes no difference if you were the bank president or the bank teller in the physical world. What matters is the quality of your life on earth. We must prepare for this journey by living on the earth with dignity, integrity, service, love, and a sense of humor.

To state it as simply as I can: At the time of death the spirit body is released from the physical suitcase. A silver cord attaches the physical body to the astral body much like an umbilical cord connects a baby to its mother. When it is time to pass over, this cord breaks. In a near-death experience the cord is not severed; the spirit body releases partially from the physical one, but the physical and astral bodies remain connected. The spirit floats above the physical body and observes what is happening around it. Clients often report this experience after surgery or at the time of a serious accident, what we call a life or death situation. Usually they hear someone pronounce them dead, whether it's the doctor in the emergency room or the police officer at the scene of an accident. Feeling as if they are floating, they can see themselves lying on the operating table, or possibly on a stretcher, and observe the activity around their physical body. Outside their body yet still in the physical realm, they can hear people trying to help them. Next, they seem to be going through a tunnel. At the end a beautiful light envelops them. Language cannot express the emotion the soul feels in this sacred vibration. Relatives and friends in spirit stand at the border and speak to them. They are told it is not yet their time to pass on. Souls who have not completed their earthly incarnation must return to the physical life. There is still work to be done.

Almost everyone who has a near-death experience returns to the body quickly. They do not have time to visit the spirit realms. But there are certain people who in their near-death experience are allowed to view parts of the spirit world. Later we will hear some of these accounts. Invariably no one wants to go back to earthly life. Don't you find this interesting?

If death is so terrible and frightening, why do people who have glimpsed the other side all tell us the same thing? "The experience was wonderful." "I have never felt such security and peace." "There is indeed an afterlife."

People who have had a near-death experience are never the same. They gain a new sense of freedom because their fear of death is gone. They understand the sacredness of life, and life takes on an even deeper meaning. They realize that the purpose of our life on earth is to learn, to grow, to improve, and to serve others.

Whenever I hear and read these stories, this part of the Twenty-third Psalm goes through my head:

"Yea, though I walk through the valley of the shadow of death, I will fear no evil."

Is it not possible that "the valley" is actually the tunnel that those who have almost passed over traveled through?

YOU WON'T BE ALONE

Despite the promise of a blissful afterlife, most human beings are frightened of taking the journey from earth to spirit. The thought of separation from our earthly friends and relatives or of missing life's joys is inconceivable. Please be comforted to know that nobody passes from the earth to the spirit alone. At the moment your spirit begins to leave your body, you will see someone standing in a shadow, extending a hand to help you cross the border. It will be a clear image of a loved one who has gone on before you. In the rare case when no one close to you has passed on, a spirit helper trained in assisting people to make the transition will be there for you.

I have been at the bedsides of many people shortly before their passing. I always know their time is close when they start telling me they're seeing people who have previously gone over. Sometimes they'll have long conversations with their mother, a grandmother, or other loved ones.

If you are not familiar with the metaphysical world, it is easy to assume that the ill person is having drug reactions or hallucinations. I assure you this is not the case. The spirit body is simply beginning to make the transition. The patient can genuinely see the spirits who are waiting for him. Being half on the earth and half in the world of spirit, the dying person begins to relate to both worlds. Just as it takes time to give birth to a soul, it takes time to leave the earth. Death is birth into the realm of the spirit.

Nicky

I kept a phone next to my bed in case my dear friend Nicky needed to talk. He and I lived in different cities and didn't see each other daily. Nicky had been seriously ill for some time and we, his friends and his family, knew that he did not have long to live. He had been released from the hospital and was with his sister. As he grew weaker, he would call me and say, "Nana is here." His grandmother, "Nana," had passed on a few years ahead of him. They had been very close and he sorely missed her.

Ten days before his passing my phone rang at three A.M.

"What are you doing?" he asked.

"Waiting for your call," I joked.

"Nana is here, but she is not close enough." He seemed a bit agitated.

"Is she saying anything to you, Nicky?"

"No, she just is here. I wish she would come closer. It is so good to see her."

"Don't worry," I comforted him, "she will come closer soon."

"Okay," he said, "that's all, good-bye."

Knowing that his time was near, I arranged to visit him at his sister's home. On my last day with Nicky on this side of life, we spoke for seven hours. He was quite weak and lay on the couch, holding my hand. The illness had taken a toll on his body. He was thin and pale and looked much older than his forty years, but he still possessed a wonderful sense of humor. With his gift for one-liners, he could make even the most horrible situation hysterically funny. That day was no exception.

"Well, if only the good die young, I guess I'll never get out of here," he joked.

I explained to Nicky that the Greeks had coined that phrase as a compliment. The Greeks knew that upon death the soul moved into a higher plane of existence and they felt that to pass over young meant that you had fulfilled your earthly duty. Their philosophy left no room for sentimentality about death. Yes, the loved one was missed, but the Greeks held the unshakable faith that all would be reunited in due time.

Becoming serious, he said, "Tell me again, Mary, what will happen when I leave this body?"

"Think of the blue Tiffany box," I told him. "Inside it there's a very special present. The box is lovely, but once you remove the gift, it's no longer needed. You throw away the box but the contents remain intact. Your physical body is the box. Your spirit body is the contents.

"When it is your time, you will feel yourself floating above your physical body. Nana will be standing so close that you'll see her extended hand. As you reach for her, you will not feel in any way lonely. You'll look down at your poor, sick body and feel amazing relief, total freedom. All your physical pain and fear will leave you instantly. It will be fascinating to look at your physical body and know for certain that it is not the real you. The voices of those around you on the physical plane will grow fainter. You will see their reactions. For a moment you will want to assure them everything is all right. Yet you realize that in time they, too, will feel this harmony. As the silver cord that attaches your physical and spirit bodies is severed, you'll move through a dark (but not scary) and tranquil space. At the end of this tunnel will be a beautiful light. You will move toward the light. Nana and other friends who have gone on before you will stand at the border to greet you. Across the border is a world of amazing beauty. You, Nicky, are fortunate, since you're already aware of life after death. Your metaphysical studies have prepared you for this journey. You will clear very rapidly."

"Clearing" means releasing any pull toward the earth plane. Faith and education make the transition much easier. Understanding the metaphysical is not a necessity, but it's helpful. Anyone who has lived a good life will also clear with little trouble.

"Your spirit friends will be rejoicing," I continued. "They won't be dressed in gloomy black. Black is saved for those on earth who still see this transformation as depressing and tragic.

"For a short time you'll feel the vibrations of the sadness of your earth friends. Though you will feel sympathy at their grief, you will lack sentiment. The knowledge that grief is a normal and necessary part of life will prevent you from worrying about the reactions of those on earth."

SEEING YOUR LIFE PASS BEFORE YOU

"As soon as the transition is made, all the events of your life will pass before you as on a fast-moving screen. You will review every episode of your life from the moment of your birth."

"Oh, no," Nicky interjected. "That's the part I just can't endure. Why must we bring up all the things we've worked so hard to forget? Looking back at my life before I saw the sacredness of it seems intolerable. I did many things that I'm not proud of."

It is important to understand that the spiritual self doesn't judge. It observes. It faces the facts. This is not an inquest. It is a recognition of actions. As you realize that the purpose of life is growth, you cannot feel guilt.

Nicky would see clearly the progress he'd made in this life, and I was certain it would make him very happy.

Surely, there are events in our lives that we wish we could change. We have eternity to improve ourselves. Reincarnation is the philosophy that teaches we live not just one but many lives. We will return to the earth until we have perfected ourselves. The soul is reborn into a new body in order to gain experience. All any of us can do at any time is our best. What our best is evolves as we learn. Physical life gives us the opportunity for this evolution. Yes, the awareness that all our actions are our personal responsibility is essential. We are accountable for every thought and every deed. Knowing this will serve to help us to *think before we act or react.* Knowing that we will have the chance to live again helps us to release the guilt of our past mistakes.

I assured Nicky: "Once on the other side, you will see you lived a life of great service to many people. It doesn't matter that you made mistakes. You must not be too hard on yourself."

Nicky had grown incredibly since our first meeting ten years earlier. It was as if he had lived two lives within one physical incarnation. When I first met him, he was lost. Life seemed to have little purpose for him. In his youth he had sought escape from the pain of his sensitive nature. But running away from himself gave him no peace of mind. The pursuit of physical pleasure had left him empty.

There is a saying: "When the student is ready, the teacher appears." I had the privilege of being first Nicky's teacher, then his friend. I introduced him to the philosophy of reincarnation and the law of karma. He embraced the teachings with passion and deep understanding. The awareness of the continuation of life (re-incarnation) and the explanation that seeming injustices are often the result of past-life karma (the law of cause and effect) gave his life meaning. It finally made sense to him. Nicky found peace through knowledge, which led him to service. If we truly understand these teachings, it becomes apparent that only through serving others can happiness be attained. He studied and became a therapist. Helping others turned out to be his passion and contentment.

Looking at him now, my realization of the truth in the words "It doesn't matter how many years you live, it matters how you live the years" comforted me.

As we hugged each other on that last day, we both knew we would not meet again on this side of life. We also knew that we would not lose touch with each other. This wasn't the end of our friendship. It was simply a change, as normal a progression as the day ending and night beginning.

"I'll see you when I get there," he laughed.

I knew that was true. My psychic gift of clairvoyance would enable me to see Nicky in spirit. I didn't need to communicate with him. I wouldn't want to pull him toward the earth. I respect a person's right to rest in peace. When we grieve too much for our loved ones who've passed over, we interfere with their ability to make a clean break from the physical world. Nicky and I had discussed this. He assured me that he would come to me if and when he needed to. Knowing my friend, he would be so busy exploring the afterlife, little time would be left to think about the physical. If something happened that he wanted to share with me, I would receive communication from him.

Ten days later Nicky suffered a mild heart attack. He called me on Thursday from the hospital and said, "I love you."

"I love you too," I replied.

"Nana seems closer. I can see her quite clearly."

"Give her my love," I replied.

"I have to go now, bye."

Those were his last words to me. Friday morning, as his parents entered his room, he sighed and left us.

HOW DOES THE SPIRIT WORLD LOOK?

My first clear view of the other side came to me when I was ten. I was sitting on the hill behind the high school in my hometown in Iowa, gazing up at the sky, when I saw what looked like a large movie screen come down in front of me. Projected on the screen was a clear picture of a world of vibrant color with people floating about in robes. Everyone seemed calm yet busy at the same time. A large Native American stood with his arms crossed in the center of the picture. (Later in life I was to learn that he was my spirit guide, White Feather.) People were moving toward a large illuminated structure that looked like a church or temple.

I had never seen color in the physical world to match what I saw on that screen. White Feather looked at me, nodded, and the picture ended.

This was the beginning of my clairvoyant connection with the other side. The more this happened over the years, the stronger the connection became.

The idea of souls wearing robes conjures up the idea of angels. To some it may seem like fantasy. Suffice it to say that common sense rules in the spirit world.

Robes are more comfortable than jeans, so most people wear them. When those in spirit come to give a message, they are usually wearing outfits that their loved ones will recognize. After their visit they return to the comfort of their robes.

It seems ridiculous to the spirit folk that they ever wore high heels or nylons or a suit and tie. The spirit body breathes and moves freely wearing robes.

In spirit we are freed from all physical problems; no one in the spirit world needs glasses to see or crutches to walk. The body is whole and in perfect health.

The physical body ages, but not the spirit body. When you see a person who was old when he passed over, he will appear to be in the prime of life. Everyone in spirit looks about thirty-five years of age, which is considered the perfect age before serious deterioration sets in. As all physical stress is removed, the person slowly restores perfect emotional balance. Part of this balance shows itself in a renewed youthfulness.

BABIES AND CHILDREN

Parents who have lost a child ask, "Will I know my baby when I pass over? If the child grows up, how will I know for certain that it is mine?"

The child will be waiting for the parents when they pass on. The child will introduce itself to the parents. Recognition will then be immediate, regardless of the age of the child. Many times the parents have had contact with their child while in the sleep state. Even if they don't remember this while on earth, the memories will come back to them in spirit.

When the soul of a child reincarnates before the passing of its parents, they are told where the child is and why the child's soul had to return to earth at that specific time. There are trained spirit therapists who talk to the parents to help them release feelings of sadness or loss.

In spirit parents understand that they create the body, not the soul of their child. The soul is eternal and must go forward with its life. Parents are temporary guardians.

A SPIRIT NANNY

It is not unusual for psychic messages to be given during the dream state. Mediums are known to speak in dream or trance conditions. The Greek oracles at Delphi induced dreamlike states by vapors. Native Americans used hypnosis, music, and other rituals to produce visions. During sleep the body is relaxed and not overloaded with the concerns of everyday life. It is easier to be open to the spirit world at those times. The astral body floats above the physical during sleep. The magnetic cord holding the bodies together keeps the connection to the physical stable.

Nevertheless, most dreams are psychological, not psychic. The only way to tell what kind of dream you have experienced is through observation and study. Write down your dreams and see if they are giving you psychic messages. Time will tell if a prediction has come to pass. Since childhood I have been given clear messages in the dream state. Not all my dreams are psychic, but I have learned to know exactly when they are. Patience and discernment have guided me well in this process.

Kathy

My friend Kathy passed over in 1988. She has appeared to me three times in dreams. Kathy came to me in the first dream just two days after her passing. Because she was still recovering from the exhaustion of her battle with cancer, she stayed for only a short time, just long enough to let me know that she was resting in a hospital. Her mother was taking care of her. You may be surprised to know that there are hospitals on the other side. These are places for rest, not medical treatment. If a person has had a very exhausting illness, a short period of rest is often needed in order to recharge the astral body. It takes a great deal of energy to leave the earth plane. Rest restores energy.

In the second dream, which came a year later, Kathy very excitedly reported her new assignment. She had been placed in charge of a large group of babies.

"I am what's known as a spirit nanny," she proudly told me. She looked radiant and her laughter was infectious. In the physical Kathy had been a registered nurse and a midwife. Her greatest love was children. There was no better person to handle this job. She would treat each of the spirit babies in her care as if they were her very own.

A few months ago she appeared in the third dream to update me on her work with the children. All was going well. The babies were growing up quickly, getting prepared for future lives on earth. She took me to view the nursery. It was enchanting. Beautiful murals of Mother Goose nursery rhymes were painted on the walls. These murals seemed alive.

I heard no crying in this realm of the spirit. Children

were singing songs and laughing. It was an amazing sight. I am certain that anyone who has had a child pass on in infancy would be overwhelmed to know the care its soul was being given.

Amazing Grace

My grandma Grace lived in the physical to the ripe old age of ninety-six. She passed into spirit on October 14, 1990. I telephoned her on October 5, her birthday.

"Happy birthday, Gram," I said.

"This will be my last birthday, Mary," she replied.

"How do you know?"

"I just know. You of all people should understand. I love you and I'll see you in heaven."

Nine days after this conversation Gram passed over in her sleep. During the year before her passing, Grandma was a bit confused. When I telephoned she would think I was my mother or my sister. But the last time I spoke to her she was clear as a bell.

Grandma Grace had never been afraid of death. She talked about it in a very natural way. She wasn't psychic and never thought in a metaphysical way. Common sense reigned in her household.

It was not until January 1993 that I saw my grandmother in spirit. She came to me in a dream, sitting in a green chair that had been in front of a picture window in her Iowa home.

"Grandma," I asked, "why do you just sit in that old green chair? There are many things for you to see in the spirit world and you are missing them. Don't you want to look at the gardens or see the art galleries?"

"I can see everything I want to from right here. I've

always loved this chair. I love to watch the people moving around. Your aunt Mayme was just here visiting me. She didn't stay long. As usual, she's busy running all over. Mayme could never sit still." (Mayme is Grandma's identical twin sister.)

My sister Sheila and I were raised by our grandma Grace. When we were little we'd always see Gram sitting in her chair, looking out the window. She worked very hard as a nurse and taking care of us. She had a wonderful garden and spent many happy hours working outdoors. She relaxed by sitting in her green chair and watching the world from her picture window. Often, she told us that when she died (the term she always used), she would rest in her green chair for as long as she liked. To her this would be heaven.

Feeling no need to explore the spirit world, Gram seemed perfectly happy. Her face looked to me like that of a thirty-five-year-old, not a line on it.

"Your uncle Dick comes by to see me every day. He is a wonderful son."

My uncle had passed on a few years before Grandma, and this loss had broken her heart. Now they were together and I knew Gram was fine. She then named all her friends who were there with her and told me what they were up to. Chatting away, she seemed just as she did when I used to run home after school, feeling a great sense of comfort just knowing that she would be sitting at the window in her green chair.

Waking up from this dream, I was positive that she would still be sitting there, waiting for me, when it was my time to move on into the spirit world.

How We Can Help People Make the Transition

Education releases fear. My instruction began in the funeral parlor owned by my great-aunt.

One day she had errands to run and could not leave the place unattended, so I was sent to answer the phone. I took this job seriously and sat staring at the phone, waiting for it to ring. Before long this became boring, so I decided to take a look around the place.

I was drawn to a room on the left of the main hallway. A wake was scheduled there later that day. Suddenly I saw a bouquet of roses and lilacs floating in the air. I remember opening and closing my eyes, expecting this apparition to disappear. The flowers continued floating. Then I saw the ever-so-faint shadow of a woman holding the bouquet. She smiled radiantly and waved. Then she replaced the flowers on a stand next to the coffin and disappeared. When I walked into the room I saw that the woman holding the flowers was the same person lying in the coffin. I was not afraid. Confirmation that death is a fantasy had been given to me. What a gift! From that day on I was certain that nothing dies. The termination of the physical body is a passage. It is a change. Leaving the physical is a metamorphosis, not a termination.

Change often frightens people. Starting a new job, moving into a new home, entering into a new relationship, fills us with apprehension. Fear vanishes once we are able to adjust to the alteration.

Preachers banging podiums, yelling about eternal damnation, have not been helpful. They have instilled fear. Simple human errors have been described as mortal sins. Death has been called the final judgment, or the grim reaper.

Parents lie to children about death. They think they're protecting their children by whispering about it or not discussing it at all.

Death should not be a secret. It should be discussed in an open, loving, beautiful manner. Just as we must teach our children manners and right from wrong, they must be taught not to fear death. Learning that change precedes growth is a lesson that will support them in all areas of life. Looking at death as a normal process—a part of life—will free children from fear. Show them the flowers and the trees and how they bloom in the spring and rest in the winter. This is a simple, beautiful, and accurate metaphor for our lives. It is our own fears that keep us from discussing the normalcy of passing on with our children.

But fear is learned. I once heard fear described as "the absence of God." This rang true to me because people who believe in a force greater than the personal self are less fearful and more able to appreciate the sacredness of life. And you don't need to believe in a personal deity or join a church to become a believer. Having a sense of the higher self that dwells inside the heart of everyone suffices. This higher self is the motivator that leads us to desire to serve others. It is the soldier that slays the dragon of fear.

Letting Go

One of our greatest tests in life is learning to let go. A mother must let her child go to live his own life. If she hangs on too long, she will have a dysfunctional adult child on her hands. It is likewise difficult for a child—even an adult of forty—to let go of the need for parental approval and dependence, or the past.

Both the parent who can't release the child and the child who can't embrace his independence must learn to love each other in a way that permits growth. To love with detachment is the key that opens the door to spiritual happiness, the key to learning to let go. Detachment must not be confused with indifference: Indifference is not caring. Detachment is caring deeply enough to separate.

Life is a continual process of letting go. Or should I say going forward?

The good teacher doesn't try to hold his students back. He is proud when they graduate to the next class. A good therapist is delighted when his patient no longer needs his services. In China a good doctor is one who keeps his patient healthy. He asks for no payment if the patient becomes ill. His duty is to give a person the tools to live with balance.

Balance

To live with balance is to live in harmony. Disharmony is the root of all problems. A balanced diet—both mental and physical—promotes energy and growth. When we feel off balance, we are being alerted that there's a problem to solve. A happy life is one with physical, emotional, and spiritual equilibrium. Excessive behavior such as overindulging in alcohol or food causes us to feel unbalanced. The law of karma teaches that for every action there is a reaction: In other words, your action will be balanced by an equal reaction. For example, if you laugh at someone's misfortune, in time you, too, will be unfairly ridiculed. Balance is wisdom.

Part of balance is learning when to let go. If we can acquire the ability to discern when it is time to let go, we will have few unhappy moments. Living for the moment brings great joy. Relishing each event frees us from the slavery of living in the past. Clinging to the past instead of going forward can be a selfish act.

Death is the ultimate test of our ability to let go. Be it our own transition, or that of our loved ones, death is the most significant forward move in our lives.

George

George is thirty-seven and lives with his mother. Though it is quite common for young people to return home after college because they cannot afford to live on their own, George has more than enough money. It's fear that keeps him tied to his mother. George is terrified that Marian, who is getting on in years, will die. Obsessed with this fear, he is miserable.

Marian came to see me. Terribly concerned about her son, she wasn't having much fun herself.

"It's my fault," she sighed. "I lied to George about his father's death, trying to protect him. He was only eight years old. It was a big mistake. If I had been honest, I think George would have been able to cope with life in a mature manner. How could I have been so unenlightened?"

When George's father died, instead of telling him the truth Marian told him that his father had gone out of the country on a long business trip. Intending to explain it to him when he was a little older and could handle it better, she left George with the cruel expectation that his father would return. Whenever George asked about his father, Marian would change the subject until she became unable to tell him the truth. When George finally learned the truth—from a school friend—he became hysterical, and thereafter he refused to let his mother out of his sight. Out of guilt, Marian allowed George to become overly attached to her. Now, thirty years later, he was completely unprepared to handle life without her.

What could Marian do to help her son?

George had tried therapy but stopped, insisting that he had no problems. His personal relationships suffered. No woman wanted to marry a man who couldn't let go of his mother.

I suggested to Marian that she get tough. Since George wouldn't move out on his own, she should force him to move, assuring him that he could visit as often as he wanted. Not surprisingly, she was reluctant to "kick him out into the streets."

But I knew that George could afford his own place, and he would be fine once he adjusted to his new home. As for Marian, it was time for her to let go of her guilt. Yes, she should have told him the truth about his father, but she had to accept that she couldn't change the past: She could only learn from it and make the present better. Helping George to let go was the first step.

The wisest deed is not always the easiest. Marian realized she could no longer continue to support George's fears. Then she made her difficult decision. She asked him to move.

A few months later Marian sounded like a new woman. George didn't leave willingly. He argued and tried to make her feel guilty, but she was steadfast.

At first he came home every day. As the weeks passed he started having a life of his own. Now he could go three or four days without seeing his mom. It had been a difficult adjustment, but mother and son are doing fine.

Loss

No one wants to lose a loved one. Parting is more often anguish than sweet sorrow. Whether it's the loss of a love affair, the loss of a dream, or the loss of a beloved who's passed over, we experience pain.

Often, a loved one passes over when no one is in the room with her. The bereaved cry and say, "I can't believe it. I left the room for only a few moments and Mother passed on. Why wasn't I there with her?"

The fact is: People making the transition to the spirit world are sometimes held to the physical world by the desire of those they love to hold on to them. The force of the grieving can make it very difficult for those who are ready to move on into spirit.

Powerful thoughts sent from the loved ones can keep people in the physical body longer than necessary. The dying can feel the sadness of people who don't want to let them go. The dying person doesn't want to hurt those who love them by leaving, so they try to hold on.

This—our desire to keep our loved ones with us—is

a major cause of physical deterioration during illness. The dying can slip away easier if their loved ones leave the room, taking their sadness with them. We must give our loved ones permission to leave us.

Throughout our lives we get many opportunities to practice the art of letting go. The ultimate act of unselfishness is to let those we love go on when their time has come.

It is not easy to say good-bye, but it is completely natural. We must realize that it is a way to free those whom we love from the bondage of physical suffering. It is an act of great dignity and service.

We must hold our loved ones and tell them that we love them and will miss them—but that we will be fine. This will help them pass on with greater ease. Put yourself in their place. Don't allow those you love to be held to the earth by their worry for you. The transition will be much easier if you give people permission to leave.

Lois

A client of mine, Lois, went into a coma. Her husband Tom called and asked me to visit her in the hospital. Sitting by her bed, I was able to psychically hear her thoughts. She was saying that she was very tired and was ready to move on but she couldn't bear to leave her grieving husband.

She begged me to explain to Tom the transition from the physical to the spirit. "If only he could understand that there is nothing to be afraid of, he wouldn't feel so anguished. My sister is waiting in the shadow for me.

She understands why it is not yet possible for me to leave."

I patted this dear lady's hand and left the room to find her husband.

I had known Lois and Tom for a long time. I knew that Tom believed in the afterlife. He just couldn't bear to lose his beloved wife of thirty years.

When I gave him Lois's message, he broke down and sobbed. "How can I go on without her? She's my best friend."

"It's only for a short time, Tom. You'll see her when it is your time to go. You don't want her to suffer any longer. Go to her, tell her that you'll be fine. She's waiting to hear that from you. She loves you so very much. It's breaking her heart to feel your pain. Her sister is standing nearby, waiting to help her make the transition. Tom, I know that you cannot bear the idea of being on earth without Lois. She loves you so deeply that she cannot leave until you give her permission to do so. This may be the most difficult action you will ever have to perform. It will also be a magnificent display of the depth of your love for her."

Tom left me to spend time alone with his dear Lois. He sat on the bed beside her. He talked about their life together. Laughing at times over the memories calmed him. Telling her he loved her and would miss her but wanted her to go on to her new life freed both of them.

He left the room to get a cup of coffee. Lois passed on while he was gone. Tom knew before he returned to the room that she was gone. Later he remarked that he had never experienced the peace he had felt as he entered the room and looked at Lois. At that moment he felt positive that she was truly in a higher place.

Get Your House in Order

An important part of the transition process is getting our physical life in order. Many people are unable to move into the spirit world because they feel they have unfinished business on earth.

My friend Beth's mother lay totally paralyzed for eight months. Unable to move or speak, she could only open and close her eyes sporadically. I visited her at her bedside. As I held her hand, I was deeply disturbed by her vibrations. Though she seemed to be in a resting state, she was deeply worried that her personal affairs were not in order. Beth's mother was a profoundly spiritual woman with no fear of the afterlife. On various occasions we had talked about our common beliefs. Knowing what a responsible person she was, it was clear to me she could not pass over until her personal affairs were settled.

Yet Beth refused to talk about her mother's will.

"I don't want to talk about it. It is morbid," she snapped.

"Beth, I've been sitting at your mother's bedside. I feel that she is distressed because she wants her affairs in order. I don't want to upset you, but I have no choice but to tell you what I perceive. We've known each other for a long time and I know your mother very well. You trust my psychic abilities. Let me help you to help your mom. It is not morbid to discuss her will. It is necessary to give your mother peace of mind."

Beth found the safety-deposit box key and got the will. There were very specific instructions from her mother about the handling of the estate. Certain things needed to be arranged immediately. As soon as she knew everything had been taken care of, Beth's mother passed on in her sleep.

If possible, be sure to have your personal affairs in order, and also make certain that those who are close to you have things arranged in a manner that will promote peace of mind.

Be direct but kind with people who you know are dying: Help them to get their things in order. Talk to them and ask how they would like their things handled. Don't wait until a person is so ill that he can't think rationally. Once the physical duties are handled, we are free to contemplate the affairs of the soul and pass on with greater tranquillity.

Lucy

Lucy's fiancé keeled over from a heart attack two weeks before their wedding was to take place. She and Henry were very much in love. They had shared his condo for two years. He had intended to put the place in her name but hadn't gotten around to it. When they decided to marry, Lucy gave up her rent-stabilized apartment. After the funeral, Lucy returned to the condo heartbroken and exhausted. Looking around at the things they had shared made her cry, yet it comforted her to be in their home.

Two weeks after the funeral Henry's adult son from his first marriage told Lucy that he wanted to live in the condo. He gave her one month to move. Stunned, she tried to explain that she had no place to go. On top of her overwhelming grief, she now felt complete despair. She arrived to see me dazed and frightened. She broke down as she told me her story. Suddenly I felt a very strong presence in the room.

"Henry is here and wants to speak to you," I said.

He was very upset and kept asking Lucy to forgive him for leaving her unprotected. He could not leave the earth sphere until he told her how sorry he was. He was shocked and dismayed at the selfishness of his son.

Lucy listened, floored but receptive. Looking over to me for strength, she told Henry not to worry. She loved him very much and wanted him to go on. She knew that he had not meant to hurt her. Lucy also asked him to forgive his son. It was important to her that he understand there was no resentment on her part.

I felt his presence for another moment, then he left us. Lucy was visibly shaken but in awe. It was a great privilege to receive the confirmation that Henry was gone yet very close at the same time. He had suffered over the disorder with his estate. Lucy, deeply saddened but stronger, went on with her life.

Think about the anxiety Henry attracted by neglecting to have his affairs in order. His sudden passing was a shock. Unfortunately, this kind of thing can happen to anyone. This is a lesson for all of us. We must always have our houses in order. How many people are left without knowing what a person wants done with his or her estate? The fights among survivors that often result are intolerable. This negativity can reach the departed soul. The soul can feel these powerful thoughts. These thoughts are very upsetting to one who has passed and prevents the soul from resting in a peaceful state.

Listen to the Dying

Listen to people who are facing the transition from earth to spirit. Give them the freedom to express their emotions. People need to talk. We must allow them to do so.

I received a phone call from an old friend who was very ill. "No one will talk about my death. The doctors have said that recovery is almost impossible. I'm not being negative, just realistic. My family will not face the possibility that I may not have much time left. Everyone is pretending that I will be just fine. The need I feel to talk is overwhelming, but seeing the faces of my family when I try to express myself stops me. Sometimes I just want to scream 'Help me! I'm the one who's dying.' " He started to cry.

"I'm here. You can tell me anything that you want to," I said. He talked for the next hour. Moments of rage alternated with laughter. Sharing his worries and fears about dying helped him greatly. I said very little. Just being on the other end of the phone, listening, was all he needed from me. Listening is a powerful tonic for one who is in pain. It's difficult to face the reality that one we love must leave us. Most of us don't want to hear about it. We're afraid—of loss, of facing our own mortality, that we will say the wrong thing, that we won't be able to bear the sadness.

We must forget ourselves and our personal feelings and fears and just listen.

We are able to show great love through the art of listening. And as we are able to comfort our loved ones, we are also being educated.

Ruthie

Ruthie's brother listened at her bedside. She kept pointing to a chair in the corner and asking if he could see the man sitting there. Robert couldn't, and he asked her to describe him. Although she was exhausted from her illness, Ruthie would perk up as she described her visitor. For three days as she went in and out of consciousness she talked about the man in the chair. Robert listened patiently and asked questions about the man. On the third day Ruthie slipped into a coma. Robert told Ruthie he loved her and gave her permission to leave. Telling her not to fear the journey, as all would be fine, he got up from her bedside. He didn't want to keep her tied to the physical by his presence.

Kissing her cheek, he moved away from her bed to look upon her for a moment. To his surprise she opened her eyes and said,

"Don't forget us."

"Us?" Robert asked.

"You know, you and me."

She then slipped back into a coma.

Eight hours later she passed over to join the man in the chair, who Robert realized was their father. Robert had been a great support. He had served her well by listening and by giving her permission to go.

Lawrence My Master Teacher

It was in April 1993 that I once again saw my dear teacher, Lawrence. I was vacationing in Edgartown on Martha's Vineyard. It was not yet the tourist season, and few people were on the streets. I was staring at a beautiful lamp in the window of an antiques store, when suddenly he was standing next to me. I was overjoyed to see him.

"It is lovely, my child. The Victorians certainly could produce the most beautiful lamps."

Overwhelmed with the surprise of seeing him, I said, "Thank goodness, Lawrence! I really need to talk with you."

"I was aware of that. This seemed like a nice tranquil place to have a chat. Let us go and sit in the little park across the way. Such a lovely spot and we will not be interrupted there."

Walking with Lawrence, my mind returned to the warm May day seven years before when I was sitting in Central Park, watching children at play, when he first introduced himself to me.

At that time I was busy writing my first book. My dear friend Kathy was very ill with cancer. Spending mornings at the hospital, afternoons seeing my private clients, and weekends writing left me little leisure time.

On this particular spring morning I awoke feeling compelled to go to the park. I realized later that it was destined that Lawrence and I meet that day. With my psychic ability I recognized him immediately as my spiritual teacher. I'd seen him in a dream when I was a little girl. After our initial meeting in the park we had many conversations. I ran into him frequently on the streets of Greenwich Village, or he'd be sitting in a booth at a coffee shop I'd gone into for lunch. He offered me his *point of view* on many issues and supported me through the difficulty of writing my first book, as well as with the passing over of my dear

friend. It was not Kathy's passing that had been so upsetting, but the personal emptiness that I felt because I
missed her. Over the course of our relationship Lawrence and I have discussed many problems and together
found solutions. He introduced me to his teacher Sir
William who also taught me a great deal.

Lawrence and I had not seen each other for three
years. I had been through some difficult times since
we'd last met, and I thought about him often, knowing
that he could feel my thoughts. There were times when
I felt I couldn't continue without physical contact with
him. At those moments a comforting presence would
envelop me. I could feel his support even though he
wasn't actually present. Knowing it was not my place
to ask him to come, I did the best I could. Faith taught
me that he would appear when he felt it was necessary,
and that he had good reasons for all his actions. It was
my spiritual test to deal with the situations that were
presented to me.

Now we were united when I was involved in writing
this book. It was as if there had been no passage of
time.

We settled ourselves onto a bench in the park and sat
together quietly for a few moments before he spoke.
"So few people are able to enjoy pure silence. There is
great peace and harmony of the spirit once we can learn
to be still."

He then proceeded to speak of all that I had done
since our last meeting. He had been aware of everything, as he was able to tune in to my thoughts. He told
me that he was sorry that I had had to get through tough
times on my own. He had been in seclusion recharging
his body. The vibration of the earth had taken a toll on

his highly sensitive nature. All teachers had to remove themselves from the turbulence of life for periods of rest. Also, he added, it would not have served my personal growth to have him with me when I needed to be learning for myself.

"The decade of the nineties will be amazing for the growth of the world. Mankind is being forced to face the fact that the materialism of the eighties did not promote lasting happiness. I can see a change of consciousness as people begin to look more toward the spiritual side of life."

Boy, is that the truth. The economy is suffering, people are losing their jobs, real estate values have dropped, health care costs have skyrocketed. Everyone is scared.

In my work as a psychic I meet people from all walks of life. Previously, no matter their status, everyone was concerned about the material future. But I've seen a change: People are asking more questions about spiritual issues. Yes, they still come to me to ask about career and relationships, but the focus of their concerns has changed. People are seeking a point of view that can support them in their daily lives.

Understanding the continuity of life helps. Physical pleasures are temporary; knowledge is eternal. Certainly, we should enjoy the material things of life. They can give us pleasure. We just can't become overly attached to them.

"That's right, my child. Things will pass, yet the God within remains eternal. People are being forced to look inside themselves to find peace of mind." He smiled.

Lawrence had once again tuned in to my thoughts.

How can I explain this great man? Lawrence had an

aura of complete serenity. In his presence I felt wrapped in a blanket on a cold winter night, safe and warm. His character was so pure that it was impossible not to be drawn to him. There was nothing intrusive in his thought reading. He knew that I trusted him completely. His bearing was aristocratic yet comfortable. He was a great sage and a wise friend.

The silence was broken by the laughter of a couple walking past us. After a few more minutes Lawrence asked if I had any questions.

"How can I better help people overcome the fear of dying? I know that there is no death. I have known that since I was a child. I realize that I have been given psychic gifts that have helped me. Seeing the other side is totally normal to me. I just wish that I could convey this to everyone."

"Just tell them what you have seen. People must first get over their fear of life, then they can work on the afterlife. It is a bit like the question What came first, the chicken or the egg?" He laughed.

"Knowledge paves the road to freedom," he continued. "Everyone must delight in the moment. Savor all experiences and relationships. Every second is important. Live live live!" He stopped and took a deep breath.

We sat together for another few minutes. His presence was a blessing. He then stood, and promising that he would be in touch in the very near future, he took his leave.

I sat alone and was suddenly aware of the aroma of roses. Looking around the park, I saw no sign of rosebushes, but to my right, on the ground, were a dozen peach-colored roses. Lawrence had left me a bouquet of my favorite flowers. I swept them up into my arms and strolled back to my hotel. Feeling giddy with happiness, and knowing that it was my job to spread our knowledge, I couldn't wait to get back to my writing.

✳ 2

We Reap What We Sow

Every action that we perform directly affects this life and our future lives. A man may commit a crime and not get caught in this lifetime. Yet his crime will not go unnoticed. It may take until the next life, but his action must be balanced. This is karma.

Karma is the law of cause and effect. It is the total of all actions in the present as well as in all preceding lives. Karma returns to each of us the results of our personal actions. We will suffer for the hurts we have inflicted and rejoice in the happiness that we have given others. Everything that happens to us reflects universal justice. Each of us lives in a place that we have earned for ourselves. This is true in the physical, mental, and spirit worlds.

Reincarnation teaches that we live not one life on earth but many. We return to the earth plane until we have achieved, through our labor, perfection. Perfection is a state of total selflessness. All desire for physical pleasures is replaced by a complete dedication to serve humanity. It takes many lifetimes to reach this state. Our karma brings us back to earth until total harmony is earned. Karma and reincarnation are integral concepts.

The individual soul chooses the pace of his growth. Some are able to free themselves from the bondage of their desires more easily than others. Once we understand that the pleasures of the physical are temporary, we are moving toward true joy, the joy that comes from knowledge. The thirst for knowledge cannot be quenched by the drinking of physical substances. Physical objects can be enjoyed, for they can possess beauty. Knowledge gained through experience shows us that to love with detachment, to enjoy without expectation, to live each moment for the love of that moment, brings man closer to pure bliss.

Stages of Evolution

Over the years I have met many people who tell me that they are living their last earth life. They take great offense when I ask them certain questions, such as:

Do you speak all languages?

Do you have complete control of your emotions?

Are you able to leave your body at will?

Is your motivation at all times completely selfless?

Have you outgrown any desire for personal gain?

Are you in perfect physical health?

These are just a few of the prerequisites for Mastership. When we have totally mastered ourselves, we no longer need to return to the earth plane. At that time all karma has been balanced, and all desires for personal gain or gratification have been transmuted into selfless motivation to serve humanity. It is not practical for us to dwell on this highly evolved state of consciousness.

Just remember, most of us have lots of evolving left to do—so pay careful attention to the lessons of this life.

All physical and emotional growth takes place on the physical plane. Each lifetime we experience is a schoolroom for the soul. Each hardship is a challenge that we face in order to work toward and ultimately achieve self-mastery. Reincarnation allows this education to continue from one life to the next. The spirit enters into a physical body in order to proceed with its evolution. The time we spend between lives varies with the individual. The more highly evolved the soul, the longer it is allowed to wait before returning to the earth plane. There are exceptions: Sometimes it's necessary for an evolved soul to return quickly to perform a job that's needed to help the world. Individual karma is involved in all phases of reincarnation. The soul's karma places it in the family, country, gender, and body type that it has earned through past life experiences or that is needed in order to go through present life tests.

There are no shortcuts to self-mastery, no easy way toward enlightenment. Much of the process is very painful. Each of us is tested by attracting experiences that we have earned by our personal choices. Pain tells us that there is a problem to solve. Life is the laboratory for the development of soul remedies. We should savor all our experiences and learn from them to make this our best life yet!

It Is My Karma

"It is my karma" is the mantra of many who refuse to accept responsibility for their personal choices. Though many things that happen to us in this life are the result of past-life actions, we must guard against using karma as an excuse for lack of good sense.

Jody

Jody kept picking married men to get involved with. Over and over she chose men who weren't free. Crying, she came to me and said, "Why must this be my karma?"

I explained to her that this was not a karmic problem, but a psychological one. She needed a good therapist to help her break the pattern. She blamed karma for her inability to make wise choices, when in reality she was in control of her choices.

"Possibly, it's your karma to be tested by your attraction to unavailable men. Once you're able to use your spiritual will to break this pattern, it will no longer be repeated. That ability will change the vibration around you, allowing you to attract a different type of relationship," I explained.

Like many people, Jody was confused about karma, believing she had to just bear her "fate." Actually, it is her karma to work to overcome her problem with men.

If you are an alcoholic, is it your karma to drink throughout the whole incarnation? Or could it possibly be your test to overcome the addiction, therefore creating new good karma? Though we can't undo past behavior, we can compensate for it: We can move forward by creating new good karma. We must overcome physical and emotional problems while in the physical body. Excessive behavior of any kind, be it drinking, over-working, or philandering, creates imbalance. Life presents us with the opportunities to balance our past actions, good or bad. If you pass over from the physical to the spirit addicted to a substance, you will reincarnate with the problem until you're able to overcome it.

Some of my wealthy clients think they've earned their wealth through past good deeds. To them I say, "Being rich isn't always a blessing. The despair of the idle rich is a common theme in therapists' offices. And the extremely wealthy often become drug-addicted because they lack values or become quickly bored with all they have. Money can be a godsend or a curse, depending upon what you do with it. You are born into circumstances that you attracted by past actions. It's your character that matters, not how much money you have. There are no banks on the other side. There is nothing wrong with living a comfortable life, but it is wrong to overlook the needs of others less fortunate. It's the karma of all of us to help anyone in need of food or shelter. There is group karma that we must all be aware of. We're each equally responsible for imbalances on the planet. Each one of us can help according to our individual circumstances. One man may help by ruling a government, another by teaching people to grow their own food, and a third by giving a needy person his old coat. The size of the contribution doesn't matter. Doing anything within your capability is enough and has a great effect. Your one act of generosity may be the impetus for a person to take control of his life."

Just as you're in charge of your own karma, you have the power to help shape the course of this planet.

Karma and Our Place in the Spirit World

We arrive into spirit in the place we have earned through our earthly actions. We must work through our physical and emotional problems on earth. Your character does not disintegrate with your physical body. You arrive into spirit the same person you were when you left your physical body, so it is wise to spend our time on earth growing as much as possible.

Some people think that once they reach the other side they are immediately full of goodness and joy. This isn't the case! A person who leaves this world angry arrives into the astral in that same condition. He will remain in this state surrounded by others who are ill-tempered until the anger dissipates. If you are consumed with jealousy while in the physical, you enter the spirit world the same way. However, a good man on earth will be a good man in spirit. He will live among other fine people.

Your character is built in the physical realm. The magnitude of this is awe-inspiring. But life doesn't terminate with the elimination of the physical shell. *Do unto others* is a very serious commandment. You will receive the same treatment you give. Starting right now, become more aware of your behavior. Thinking before we act will help us to make wiser choices.

Knowing that spirit life is a continuation should be comforting. We must take personal inventory of our behavior if we do not feel the comfort.

OLD SOULS VERSUS NEW ONES

There is a myth that the older the soul, the more spiritually developed you are.

To many, a number of incarnations implies some sort of guaranteed progress. But we must not forget that many people repeat the same pattern from life to life, while others learn the first time out that fire burns. The number of incarnations is not important. How you use them is the key.

The motive behind our deeds is the key to soul development. Some are fortunate to learn this earlier than others, thus needing fewer physical lives in order to master themselves. Different souls have different aptitudes. Everyone will learn in his or her own time.

White Feather

A spirit guide is not a Master, he is a bodyguard. It is his job to protect his charge and oversee many aspects of the psychic work. Not everyone has a spirit guide. All psychics and mediums have spirit protection. Since Native Americans are considered experts in the psychic area, they are often chosen to protect those in the spiritual work. It is a great honor to be given the name of your guide. The guide doesn't take the role of a teacher but one of protector and connector. He protects the psychic from negative influences when possible and helps with the connection between earth and spirit.

The Native American who appeared on the screen in my first clairvoyant vision of the other side has been with me ever since. Later I learned that his name was

White Feather. With his help I have been shown many sides of the spirit world. I have visited the spirit realms with him often during sleep. Yet during my waking hours visions of the astral often come to me in flashes on my astral screen. Time has no measure. The picture remains in my vision a few seconds or a few minutes. It seems unearthly, yes, but it is very real at the same time.

I have never been afraid of my psychic experiences. Never. Is the artist afraid to put brush to canvas? Fear arises only when the love of the art becomes competitive, or if we are taught to be afraid.

As a child, riding my blue Schwinn deep into the country on very hot summer days made me happy. I would find the perfect spot in the shade and sit, comfortable in my own company. I perceived myself as a bit of the mystic. At these very special times, the visions came with great clarity, and my large Native American friend was always in the picture.

Reading my journals from this period, it is evident that I understood reincarnation and karma yet lacked the precise words to define these philosophies.

It was in my twenties that I first learned the name of my guide. He was standing in my living room next to the blue chair that I always sit in when I do my psychic consultations. Arms folded across his chest (the same pose he took when I first saw him at the age of ten), he impressed his name upon my mind clairaudiently.

In my head I heard a strong, clear, precise voice. "I am White Feather. If you need me, invoke my name. I will never be far from you, for it is my duty to watch over you. I have followed you since your birth."

Having known him since childhood, I nodded in reply with reverence. I had never needed a name for him, but it enhanced our connection when I could identify my friend and spirit companion by his name.

Remember, these events were completely normal to me. They were, to quote Carson McCullers, "the we of me," such a part of my life that there was no separation. White Feather and I were one.

White Feather was always impressing me with helpful messages. He is still always present during my visits to the astral plane. Arms crossed, looking completely calm, he has guided me through all my journeys.

More than once he has saved my life. Crossing a busy New York intersection, an invisible arm grabbed me, rescuing me from an out-of-control taxi. People standing on the curb gasped as I literally flew backward out of the range of the vehicle. I joked with a frightened bystander, "I guess I have a guardian angel." She made the sign of the cross and mumbled. Thanking White Feather, I vowed to be more careful crossing streets.

Once while in Santa Fe, a group of friends and I were to fly to Nevada in a private plane. The night before the planned departure, I was told by my guide not to fly in that plane. Knowing that the pilot would be upset, I told his wife, my girlfriend, that we must not go, as there was a problem with the aircraft. She had no trouble accepting my decision, but her husband, ranting and raving, insisted that there was nothing wrong with the plane. He said he had just had it serviced. They proceeded to have a terrible argument, wherein he accused her of being overly influenced by my psychic powers. For the next hour he listed all the things he found wrong with her. He used this incident to vent his anger about everything. His negativity upset her to the point that she became ill and ended up in the hospital.

Arriving at the hospital, I saw her husband in the waiting room. The doctor said that my friend wanted to see me. Not knowing what had happened, I entered her room. Reporting the incident, my friend said that she would never go back to her husband. They had been unhappy for a long time, and this scene brought everything to a head.

I stayed with her until she felt like napping. When I left the room, her husband approached me, looking very remorseful. It seemed that he had had the airplane checked again and there was a leak in the gas line. Had we taken off, odds were we would have gone up in smoke. Apologizing profusely for his behavior, he thanked me for saving our lives. In this case White Feather not only saved our lives, but my girlfriend's sanity. She had been afraid to leave her husband, and this incident had been the catalyst to give her the strength to move on with her life. Her husband was not an evil man. He was very difficult for her and they were completely incompatible. Both of them are much happier now. And I am sure that he always double-checks his airplane.

Certainly not all my psychic messages come from hearing the voice of my guide in my head. It's comforting to know that he is nearby and will speak when he feels it is needed.

White Feather not only protects but he connects as well. During some sessions with my clients I receive vivid pictures of someone whom they love who has passed on. Picking up my thought form, White Feather goes to the realm that the spirit is residing in. He informs the spirit that he is needed for a few minutes, then helps me to focus on the person. This happens only when it's the karma of the person on earth to be given a message. The loved one in spirit respects this and is happy to be of service.

I never try to bring souls to the earth unless they wish to come. Most people who have passed on are very busy in the spirit world. Once they have left the earth's sphere, they have little desire to reconnect to the physical plane. It is selfish and disrespectful to try to force those who have gone on to come to us because we're unable to let go.

Yes, there are times when it happens because it is necessary and helpful. It is not my decision, I merely deliver the message. White Feather is very helpful at these times.

Karma is the key. It is some people's karma to have a near-death experience so they can tell us about it or so they can understand the sacredness of life. It is also karmic when one is allowed to give or receive a message from the spirit world. A mother may be allowed to know that her son who passed on in a war is fine and at peace. A man who accidentally killed someone may be allowed to tell the departed that he is sorry. Earlier I told the story of Henry coming to tell Lois that he was sorry. He had earned the right to deliver this message through me.

Bill

Joan did not believe in psychics. I had gone to her home to see a friend of mine who was having a business meeting. When I entered the house I was overwhelmed by the smell of cigarette smoke, although no one was smoking. Seated in the den, I tried to be pleasant even though I was having trouble breathing because of the smoke. My friend Sue had been very clear. Joan was not interested in anything psychic. In fact, she thought all psychics were frauds. Nonetheless, as I sat waiting I could feel a cold breeze, a familiar feeling that told me a spirit was present. Then I saw White Feather standing in front of me. I couldn't see anyone else but I could feel them. The room seemed to become more smoke-filled, choking me. Still trying to be the perfect guest, I said nothing but concentrated on White Feather.

My friend came into the den with Joan, and we all made polite conversation. To my surprise, Joan started asking questions about my work. I was having trouble answering her questions because I kept hearing someone say, "Tell her that Bill is sorry that he smoked so much. Also that he is worried about their daughter's irregular heartbeat."

I was facing a dilemma. I didn't want to push this phenomenon on Joan, yet I didn't want to neglect Bill. The fact that White Feather was there made me feel more confident. Nothing ventured, nothing gained—I gave Joan the message.

She began to cry, not from sadness but from overwhelming emotion. My friend Sue told me they had just been talking about Bill's death. He was a three-pack-a-day cigarette smoker. Joan felt his habit had caused his heart attack. She had always been angry at him for leaving her and the children too soon.

Visibly shaken, Joan said to me, "No one knows about my daughter's problem. She told me about it just yesterday. I can't believe this."

I began to worry that I had not made the right choice. I had decided to respect Bill's need to get his message across. I had no intention of shocking or frightening Joan. Psychic phenomena can be unbalancing if one is not prepared to experience it. I never try to force messages upon anyone. I had been warned about Joan's attitude, but here I was in her home, giving her direct messages from her dead husband.

Let me say that I was delighted when the smoke cleared (physically as well as emotionally). Joan dried her eyes and seemed genuinely happy. Her anger toward Bill began to leave her.

No longer a nonbeliever, Joan now has a very healthy respect for the metaphysical. In my subsequent visits to her home, I didn't see or smell any signs of Bill. He had gotten his message across and didn't feel the need to return. I was thankful, as I knew this meant Bill was at peace now. He had karmically earned the right to tell his wife he knew his smoking had shortened his life. Also he was able to show his concern for the family. I had been given the privilege of conveying the message.

Lawrence Speaks to Me About Karma

Walking down Bleecker Street, softly singing my favorite song, "Night and Day" by Cole Porter, I heard someone join me. When I turned around, I was truly surprised to find Lawrence. Even more surprising was his professional-sounding voice. I had no idea that he could sing or that he would even want to. He had once told me that his mother had been very musical, but he never mentioned anything about his own ability. There was clearly a good deal that I did not know about this great man. He, on the other hand, knew a great deal about me.

"Singing is good for the soul. It can be very balancing to and relaxing for the nervous system. That is, if one can just enjoy doing it for the love of the act. You, my child, were not aware that I had heard you singing in nightclubs when you were doing the cabaret scene," he laughed.

"You were there and I didn't see you? I can't believe that." I hadn't sung professionally for at least twelve years. I was shocked.

"It seems that your karma changed in midstream. A bit like changing hats," he added.

During my early years in New York, fresh out of college, I passionately pursued a career in music and drama.

As a small child I had loved singing and acting. Performing came very naturally to me. I also possessed the ability to see fairies and elves as well as human spirits, so I never lacked an audience. In the backyard of my Iowa home I performed for my spirit friends on many occasions.

Grandma Grace would come out to weed her garden and ask, "Who in the world are you talking to?"

"Just some friends," I would tell her, continuing my performance.

After I finished college, I arrived in New York with a great deal of enthusiasm and very little money. I'd always felt destined to live there, and now I felt that I was finally home. The reality of having to pay the rent forced me to do various jobs while I pursued my theatrical career.

Singing in cabarets and piano bars was a source of income and experience. I loved performing, but I always felt that there was something missing.

During one nightclub engagement, as I was finishing my last set, Judy Garland suddenly appeared at a corner table. I had been sitting on a stool in front of the piano, where I could see everyone in the audience, and I was certain she had not been there earlier. Judy sat very respectfully and listened. There was an unearthly vibration surrounding her. How I kept singing with this great talent visiting me from the astral realm is a mystery. She had been in spirit for quite a few years, yet her great gift lived on. Her work had always been an inspiration to me. As I finished my final song I watched as she faded from sight.

That was the last time I sang professionally.

I fell asleep that night and Judy came to me in a dream. She told me that I sang well but could help people more by doing my psychic work full-time. I'd given many people advice based on my psychic awareness, so I had no trouble attracting a private clientele.

As I pursued my new career, the feeling that something was missing left me.

"I was there the night you saw Judy Garland." Lawrence broke the silence.

"That makes perfect sense to me now," I added.

"It was your choice, my child. I am very glad that you decided to change careers. No one would have pressured you to do so. It was your karma to choose."

"Lawrence, I have never regretted my decision for one moment. As you heard, I still get a kick out of singing. It's enough for me to sing for my own pleasure.

But it's not often that I have the honor of being joined by someone as musical as you."

Laughing, he invited me for a cup of coffee. We were shown to a quiet table in a nearby espresso bar.

"Just like old times," I said.

"I told you that we would meet again soon." He patted my hand.

A woman bumped into our table and excused herself. Looking up, I felt sad for her because she had a serious birthmark covering most of her face.

"That's quite all right, my dear," Lawrence assured her. The smile she gave him lit up the room.

After she was out of earshot I said, "Must be very difficult karma for that young woman."

"No, she is at peace with herself. It's evident by the way she smiles and looks one directly in the eye. I am sure she had parents that loved her and gave her the tools to cope with her imperfection. She has great soul beauty. Anyone who spends time with her will see the inner person. She has served others by her dignity and lack of self-pity." He paused and looked over at her.

"Yes, it was her karma to incarnate with this birthmark. It is her personal choice as to how she deals with this. Her behavior is creating new good karma every moment. Remember, everything is karma.

"No one enters physical life problem-free. What would be the point? Each of us has his or her karmic tests. Once the test is presented, free choice reigns. One man may be born a cripple and live angry and curse the Almighty for this malady. Yet another crippled man may be grateful that he is not blind or deaf. The soul development will shine through." He stopped as the waiter came by for our order.

"No rational man can deny that physical life is temporary. Physical problems pass. The soul retains a memory of all our lives, all our actions. This record is the road map for our present life and future lives. This map shows us various routes that we can choose in order to arrive at our final destination." He paused again.

We talked about how often people confuse karma and predestination, and use them as excuses for not overcoming challenges in life—how people don't understand that it's their karma to overcome problems rather than accept them. We went on to discuss the difficulty of proving these intangible concepts.

"The materialist will believe nothing that he cannot prove by the use of his five senses. How can we prove to the deaf man that music exists?" Lawrence interjected.

"Lawrence, my philosophy is that no matter what one believes, he will in time discover the truth. Is it wise to try to convince people that life is eternal?" I asked.

"Each of us is given a special talent in life. One man can play the piano well, thus giving others many hours of pleasure. A good doctor doesn't study medicine for years merely to treat his own body. Many souls would have been denied years of physical growth had penicillin not been discovered and shared with the world. You have had numerous psychic experiences and visions. What would it serve to keep these to yourself? Sharing your reflections of life on the other side will help many to overcome their fear of the unknown. All you can do is offer your insights. Do not worry about reactions. If it were not your karma to present your knowledge, you would not have chosen this work. You could have lived a nice life as a singer and an actress." He again sipped his coffee.

The woman with the birthmark waved as she left the café.

"There goes a remarkable soul," Lawrence said. "In her next life she will have no birthmark."

As Lawrence spoke, he appeared to be in another world. I knew what he was doing. I often did the same thing.

"Reading the akashic records?" I asked.

"How clever you are," he joked.

The akashic records hold the complete memory of all our incarnations. In order to check past-life experiences, one has to look into this astral record. This takes a great deal of concentration. You feel as though you're breaking through a wall to reach this information. I'm not always able to read these astral documents. Lawrence could do so at will.

"In time, this will become easier for you to do. It's like any art—one must practice in order to become proficient. You're able to see as much as is needed at this time. Past-life readings aren't always helpful. Our present life is the important stage of development. Mankind would have been given a more developed memory if it was important to remember all lives. Most souls have a difficult time recalling last year, and it's virtually impossible to reconstruct the events of the first year of life," he said.

"Of course, the inability to remember is the most compelling argument for the skeptic who thinks if he doesn't remember, then it could not have possibly happened.

"If the deaf man cannot hear music, it shows us only

that not all people have the ability to hear. There have been many accounts of past-life memory. Buddha saw all his lives clearly. Many people may report a clear past-life experience. Some psychiatrists are accepting the probability of past-life issues in treatment. They are recognizing that certain phobias and other psychological problems stem from earlier incarnations," Lawrence reflected.

"Reincarnation and karma cannot be separated," I said in reply. "Rebirth gives us a definite reason for the visible injustices that life seems to present. Karma gives rationality to the seemingly irrational. What would be the point of struggle if this were the only life? I could not bear seeing the heartbreak of humanity if I did not know in my soul that life is eternal. All suffering, no matter how horrible, will pass. All goodness will promote happiness. Sooner or later balance is destined." I spoke with passion.

"As one learns to understand karma, life is enriched. We are given many opportunities to improve ourselves. The earth draws us to itself in order to provide the possibilities for this. Pain can be lessened through knowledge. Now, my child, it is my karma to have to leave you at this time," he joked.

"It is my karma to have to deal with your leaving." I tried not to look sad.

I was always overcome by a feeling of loss after these meetings with Lawrence. As I looked at him, he radiated a healing power, filling me with gratitude for the privilege of his company.

He walked me to a taxi and we said good-bye. As the taxi pulled away, I turned to wave and he was gone.

The karmic bond between Lawrence and me is very

intense. I've always been positive that this was not our first life together.

That night at home I quietly meditated by candlelight. As I stared at the flame, a clear picture of the pyramids passed in front of me. The vision may have lasted for a few seconds or minutes. Time stood still. I saw Lawrence dressed in ancient clothing, waving to someone to come over to him. When the figure turned its head toward me, I saw a face that clearly resembled my own. Eventually, the image faded and I was aware of my physical surroundings again. The flame had burned out. Beyond a shadow of a doubt I knew that Lawrence and I had been together in a prior incarnation in Egypt. I would ask him about it when we next met.

A desire to hear Judy Garland sing came over me. Going to the music cabinet, the evening twelve years before, when I had seen her, came to my mind. All accounts that I had read about her life portrayed a soul in torment. It was comforting knowing that she had found a place of peace on the other side. She wouldn't have been able to visit me if she were not in a state of calm. She had served us while on earth through her magnificent talent. In spirit she had served me through her guidance. Tonight her music would calm my soul.

Short-Memory Syndrome

It's true that most of us are not capable of recalling our past lives. But this does not give us permission to have a short memory—to not learn from past experiences.

If you forget the past, you'll repeat mistakes and patterns, ultimately driving yourself into a karmic frenzy.

Your karmic pattern changes once you have faced the lesson that has been presented and have taken positive action to overcome any obstacle to your spiritual growth. Remembering how we felt or acted in any situation will help our lives to flow more smoothly. For instance, if you keep losing jobs or friends or lovers because you have an ego problem, you won't have a happy relationship until you face the problem, take action, and overcome it.

Lionel

Lionel arrived in New York from Ohio desperate to break into the clothing business. He was employed as a salesperson at a large men's store. Even with no prior experience he was able to get this job. However, within two weeks he had managed to alienate everyone he worked with. Because he acted as if he were better than everyone else, he was fired. His second job, also in sales, ended in the first week, after he spoke to no one and refused to take direction from the manager who "knew nothing." This pattern continued through the loss of four more jobs. Finally, Lionel, desperate to find work, came to me for a consultation.

He spoke of his frustration working with people he considered "common." His condescension was amazing. He didn't have a kind word for anyone.

I felt a great deal of pity for him, sensing his low self-esteem was buried beneath his self-righteousness. His employers wouldn't be interested in his psychology. Though if he wouldn't change his attitude, there was little hope he could keep a job.

I pointed this out to him and predicted he would keep getting fired if he failed to learn from past experiences.

"Lionel, can't you see the pattern?" I asked.

"Yes, everyone that I work with is stupid," he snapped.

"Well, they have a job and you don't. Obviously, there's a problem. Do you think that you're difficult to work with?" I asked.

"I wouldn't be if I were working with equals," he retorted.

"Lionel, how did you become so judgmental? Have you taken the time to get to know anyone whom you work with? Certainly, they're people who you could be friends with. You have a spiritual test in front of you. You must learn humility. The jobs that you are attracting are giving you the chance to learn this. Once you are able to be humble, a job that you feel dignifies you will be presented. This may seem difficult, but it's your attitude that is troublesome. It's much easier to be kind than to be angry." I paused.

I was quite surprised when he said, "I'll try. I can't stand these low-level jobs. But if that's what I have to do to make it, then I'll do it."

I assured him there are no low-level jobs, just low-level attitudes. All work is important, and you'll get what you earn. I urged him to remember why he'd been fired, and to change his behavior at work.

He left the session on his way to yet another job interview. Hopefully, he would become aware of the negative effect he had on people, so he'd be able to hold down a job. Lionel suffered from short-memory syndrome. Repeating the same behavior over and over again, never learning from his past mistakes, he was stuck in his own karma. Breaking this pattern would be painful because he would have to face his own lack of self-esteem. It could very well take more than one life for him to do this. The choice was his. He had taken a step toward change when he made the effort to talk with me.

It would take discipline for Lionel to stay employed. He would have to force himself to be polite. Once his behavior became natural, he would find a peace that he had been unaware existed. At that time his karma would change and new opportunities for growth would be presented to him.

KARMIC BONDS

Will we know each other in our future lives? How will I recognize my friends if they do not look the same? Have I known my husband before?

Many of our friends and relatives have been with us before. Your husband in this life may have been your brother or your uncle in a previous incarnation.

A mother might have been a sister in another lifetime. Some bonds between people go beyond rational or emotional. These are karmic. These bonds are not always the romantic, idealized, loving relationships depicted in New Age movie themes.

Sondra

After dating Peter for three weeks, Sondra decided to call it off. She told him kindly yet firmly that she wasn't interested in their relationship. He didn't react violently to this news. He merely started to follow her everywhere she went. Although this sort of behavior some-times is caused by obsession or other psychological is-sues, in this case it turned out to be karma.

Normally a mild-mannered person, only with Sondra was Peter unbalanced. He followed her for two years. Though he never threatened her with physical violence, his presence unnerved her. When her friends spoke to him about this, he would explain that it was his "job to protect her. I cannot leave her alone." No amount of reasoning would shake his belief that it was his mission to protect her. Because he never harmed her, the police could not intervene.

Sondra came to me in a panic, begging for advice. As she sat in front of me, I saw a very clear picture of a past life in Greece. Though I had never met or seen even a picture of Peter, I was able to give an accurate description of him. In Greece Peter was a guard in the king's army and Sondra was the daughter of the monarch. It had been Peter's job to guard this girl, but he had been lax in his mission and the girl had been mur-dered. The grief and guilt were overwhelming to him still.

Sondra looked at me as if I were slightly crazy. "That's great. But what do we do about it now?"

I told her we had to make Peter understand that he was reacting to a past-life experience. If my reading was accurate, his subconscious would recognize it im-mediately and his mission would end.

Sondra brought Peter over and I told him the story. He listened politely, and after the session Sondra hap-pily reported that he was no longer following her. It has been two years now, and he has not returned. His sub-conscious memory accepted the past-life reading. He was able to release the guilt of having failed his duties. This set Peter free and thus Sondra, too, was freed.

It's rare that I am given this type of information. We must be careful not to use karma as a way to escape responsibility for our behavior. Karma can't be ignored, but it must not keep us from looking at our problems from a rational or emotional viewpoint.

People don't usually reincarnate with the same physical looks. The personality and the astral body dissolve when the soul is ready to return to earth. Your sex changes according to the lessons the soul needs to go through. Sometimes a male body is needed and other times a female one must be entered. Obviously, if it's your karma to be the mother of an incarnated soul, you need a female body. If you are to be a great opera tenor, a male body is useful. Common sense governs.

Sometimes a particular soul has been male for a number of previous incarnations, but now it is necessary to be female. The transition can be difficult. In these cases the person may seem to be very masculine as the incarnating ego retains many memories from its past lives. This can also work in the reverse. An effeminate male may have been female for ten previous lives, thus the transition into the male body is uncomfortable.

Some people meet and feel as if they have always known each other. Often they have been together in past lives and their karma has allowed them to be reunited.

Gail and Eric

Gail and Eric met on a trip to Italy. Each was traveling alone. They kept running into each other in Venice. After the third time this happened they decided to have dinner together. Both had been drawn to Italy since childhood; both studied Italian in school and it came easily to them. Gail went to every Italian movie that played in New York and craved only Italian food. Eric's father gave him the trip because Eric refused to go on to college unless he could return "home," as he called Italy. They were both amazed at how familiar everything seemed in a country they had never visited before. Both shared the same recurring dream: They were in Venice, looking for someone they could not find. They spent the rest of the trip traveling together through the country of their dreams. Back in New York, they married, completed their education, and moved to Italy. Eric is a writer for an Italian newspaper and Gail works in a museum. I have never met two happier people. Is it karma? I would say definitely so!

We have all lived many lives and have met many people on our journeys. Our souls are reconnected when there is a karmic reason.

If you have caused a person grief or harm, you will be forced to face this person again. If you have given love and joy, this will be returned to you. Your higher self knows everything. It is this part of ourselves that creates our individual lives. This divine self returns to the earth in order to earn freedom. There is no external personal God standing in the heavens judging our actions. Our actions judge themselves.

Karma and reincarnation alienate no one and no religion. It doesn't matter if you are Christian, Jewish, Hindu, Muslim, Buddhist, or any other religion. What matters is how you live. Your place in the afterlife is earned through your actions in this one. You are not separated by race, sex, or religious differences. Belief in the afterlife is not necessary, but it is a support. It helps us to make the transition more easily. The more aware a person is, the more he or she is able to experience. People who believe need little rest after making the transition. They're too excited to pause for rest. Nonbelievers, however, need time for adjustment. Often, they will remain in a sleep-type state for a period of time. This isn't bad, it's just not as fulfilling: The man who sleeps through the movie wakes up rested but has missed the experience.

Each life gives us many opportunities to improve ourselves. It is exciting and exhilarating to savor every moment of our lives. This applies both to the physical and spirit worlds. Now it is time to visit some of the spirit realms.

✳ 3

Heaven

Heaven is traditionally thought of as a place of supreme happiness, a spiritual state of everlasting communion with God. God is alternately defined as the supreme reality and as love. It follows that heaven is the place of love.

The place I'll call heaven is a place you arrive into if you have earned it through your actions. A loving person earns his place in heaven, the home of the loving, through living a good life while on earth.

Licking an ice cream cone on a hot afternoon, driving through the mountains, holding close the person you love, listening to your favorite music, gazing at a great work of art, completing a difficult project, or resting on the beach are just a few things that might make us feel heavenly.

Ten different people will give you ten different examples of their heaven. For Terry it would be an afternoon exploring antiques stores followed by a candlelight dinner with her husband. Mort finds heaven observing the stars through his telescope, whereas for Lee, winning a tennis match would be ideal. Ellen wants to lose ten pounds without dieting, and Joe simply wishes to find and marry the girl of his dreams. Money is all Clifford wants, while Shari thinks "the perfect job" would make her happy. For Leslie, who has cancer, perfect health would be her heaven. And Michael desires peace of mind.

Just as beauty is in the eye of the beholder, so, too, is the concept of heaven. As we change, so does our idea of what is heaven. A child may perceive heaven as all the candy he can eat, a teen as being accepted by his peers, a grandmother experiences the divine in the doctor's pronouncement "You're in perfect health."

One man's heaven may be another man's hell. A person who can't tolerate structure finds no peace in a corporate environment where his creative nature is strangled: His freedom is more important than financial security. On the other hand, the security minded would not be comfortable with the life of an entrepreneur. Better to make less money knowing it is stable than to live with risk. Similarly, a woman who is terrified of living alone might stay in an unfulfilling marriage because it is preferable to chancing a life without a mate.

Grandma Grace, a loving woman, found happiness sitting in her green chair, resting. To her this was and is heaven. Through her earthly actions she earned the right to rest in peace in the manner she found most pleasing. Passing over to the spirit world without fear, she was able to do just what she wanted—to sit in her favorite chair and watch everything going on around her. In time, when she's ready, she can choose to experience other parts of the spirit world.

Meanwhile, her twin sister, Aunt Mayme, is busy exploring everything there is to see in the spirit world. Mayme passed over many years before Grandma, but when she was alive Grandma had always commented about Mayme's restlessness. This trait carried over to the spirit world as well: For Mayme, spending all her time sitting on a chair would be torture, though to Grandma it's divine. They're each able to live in spirit as they choose.

Devachan

"Devachan" is the Sanskrit word for "heaven," also known as "the place of the gods."

People of good character go to devachan, a "state of consciousness" between earth lives. The time one spends there between earth lives varies, depending on individual karma.

In devachan you're surrounded by those whom you knew on the earth plane. Since it's a heavenly state of living, you are able to see whomever you choose and do what pleases you the most, removed from the problems and the pain of physical life. One's state of bliss would be interrupted if we were involved with the issues of our loved ones still in physical life.

For example, the father who passes over leaving his wife to deal with their teenage son would have no peace if he were observing the problems of his family. He can't change anything since he's not there. We do indeed "love beyond the grave"; we just don't love in an unproductive way. Instead, we love in a truly selfless manner, where understanding replaces sentimentality. The father understands that the loved ones he left behind must experience their lessons, their karma. In time they will be reunited. Remember, common sense rules in the spirit world. If you can't change a situation, don't dwell on it: Move on. It is with this in mind that we will move on to look at various realms of the spirit world.

REALMS

As a child I was told of heaven, hell, purgatory, and limbo. Heaven was where God lived, and where all good people lived with angels and music. Hell was an awful place of fire and demons. Limbo was where unbaptized babies lived. I was haunted by images of babies floating in space between earth and heaven. I couldn't understand how babies could be made to suffer for the lack of a ceremony.

Fortunately, these misunderstandings began to clear up by the time I was seven. A very different vision of the afterlife was given to me through my clairvoyance, which enabled me to focus on the astral plane. The spheres we call heaven, or devachan, were amazing. Seeing the lower spheres, or hellish ones, was and still is very upsetting to me.

OVERVIEW OF HEAVEN

There are many different realms in devachan. We earn our place through our spiritual development and character. It's like climbing a ladder. Each rung brings us closer to the top. Some climb slowly and with fear, others quickly and fearlessly. Eventually, everyone arrives at the peak. The process is the key. Each step bringing us closer to total happiness should be savored. As Lawrence has said many times, "Why rush? We have eternity in front of us."

It's hard to describe what you'll find as you enter the realms. First you'll see people you love waiting for you at the border. Their excitement is infectious. It's an honor to show new people the beauty that awaits them in devachan. The colors are stunning. Everything is so much more vivid and brilliant than it is on earth. Each part of the spirit world seems totally alive. Imagine, a world with no decay, no illness, and no negativity.

The gardens everywhere are lush and exotic and seemingly endless. The only comparable gardens I've seen on earth are at Findhorn in Scotland and at Sir William's (Lawrence's teacher) country estate.

When I first visited Findhorn, I was overwhelmed by the roses, the size of cantaloupes, which bloomed far longer than any other roses I'd seen. Findhorn is a truly remarkable, magical place. Eileen Caddy, a lovely woman with a special gift of mediumship, was given the guidance to bring Findhorn to life. Eileen had received spirit messages instructing her to communicate with "nature spirits"—brownies and fairies, who taught her how to enhance her gardens. It was an experiment that worked wonderfully, and for me it was very exciting to experience the mystery of Findhorn.

Every type of flower and tree I've ever seen fills these startlingly beautiful astral gardens.

The rivers in spirit are of the purest water; each drop shines like a diamond. Each realm is divided by a body of water. As we grow spiritually, we move to a higher realm. The higher the realm, the clearer the water. The brightness of light intensifies as we move up the ladder of soul development.

This growth takes place in the physical world. When we become a finer person in the physical, we pass on into a finer spirit realm. *Remember, our place in heaven is created by our earthly actions.*

There's a great deal of activity in devachan. You'll be drawn toward the activity of interest to you. For example, if you wish to learn more about your earthly profession, there are teachers in spirit. Instruction is readily available.

There are neighborhoods with perfect houses brought over by those who wish to continue living in them. It's comforting to many to be in a spirit replica of their earthly home. (Grandma Grace is one of many living in a house.)

Heaven is a continuation of your mental state when you pass over. You may have a house if you wish to, though it isn't necessary. The choice is yours. This being the land of no decay, the spirit houses need no upkeep. They exude natural charm.

ART GALLERIES

The original paintings for all the paintings ever done on earth are hanging in the astral galleries. In the physical world it's not possible to create the "real" work of art because we, in the physical, do not possess the tools to translate the thought onto canvas. Everything is first created in spirit, then transferred to the physical world. Inevitably, something is lost in the process. This is a difficult concept, but it will be very clear when you see the great works of art hanging in devachan. There are familiar paintings, for instance, Monets and Gauguins— yet they will appear startlingly different, alive with passionate energy. The colors are more intense than those of the earth, and in spirit works of art don't disintegrate as they do in the physical. It's very exciting to see masterpieces unharmed by time.

Maxfield Parrish has always been one of my personal favorites. White Feather has helped me to find his works. (The galleries are so enormous that you need assistance in locating specific works.) I had to learn to focus my astral screen on the works of Parrish. I'd never seen such an intense blue as the Parrish blue in spirit.

I enjoy sitting in art museums, looking at paintings. It gives me a sense of quiet peace, a spiritual comfort knowing I am in the vibration of greatness or godliness. Seeing the art in spirit, I know that inspiration is born from this realm, that ideas are conceived in spirit and channeled through those on the earth who had earned the needed talent. Many physical lives are necessary to perfect great talent.

Outside the spirit galleries, many people are busy working on various forms of art. I saw teachers examining the artists' works, and helping them. It made sense to me that the art instruction occurred in the aura of the galleries. This aura enhanced the passion of inspiration by its beauty. The students could look at the great works and learn from them.

Education continues beyond the grave. You need not study, you can merely observe the work. There's never enough time on earth to learn things that interest us because we're so busy with the affairs of the body. Since this is not the case in spirit, we can work or observe with no interruption. Many famous artists share their knowledge with others, though some artists opt to work in relative seclusion. As the spirit artist creates, thought forms can be sent to talented receptive people in the physical world.

This is one of the reasons that certain artists are compared to famous artists who have passed on. It's not always a matter of copying or being influenced by their works in the physical world (though example is a great teacher). Most great productions of any kind are a synthesis of many lives of preparation as well as astral inspiration.

LIBRARIES

White Feather has also shown me the libraries, where millions of books stretch farther than the eye can see. All original manuscripts reside here, as well as the *real* history of everything that has ever happened.

In the physical realm, historians record their own interpretations of events. One may write a description of a battle quite differently from another reporting the same historic incident. In the astral there are books that report *exactly* what happened, not someone's opinion of what occurred. This is bliss to the historian who has spent his life trying to reconstruct the past.

You may read a detailed account of the lost continents of Mu or Atlantis. The battles of Napoleon, the court of Arthur, Merlin's place in the history of England, and the final moments in the life of Sitting Bull are just a few of the volumes sitting on the shelves. Imagine being able to read about anything that interests you. (There are certain books available only to those who have earned the right to read them. These books that reside in the higher realms wouldn't be understood by the neophyte.) Of course, you don't have to do or read anything you don't want in the realms of the heavenly. No one will judge your literary choices or artistic tastes.

You reside in the place that you have earned. Those who deserve peace will not be disrupted. As each one of us has different ideas of happiness, we are given many choices.

Molly

Molly passed over from heart problems a few months ago. Born with a congenital heart weakness, Molly always knew she wouldn't live a normal lifespan. She was in no way a negative person—she was merely pragmatic. She had survived risky surgery three times. I first met her shortly after her last operation.

She entered my apartment breathless and very excited, and I was struck by her fiery red hair. She thanked me for seeing her on such short notice. She'd told me that it was an emergency, so I fit her in right away.

"I don't quite know how to begin," she said with great intensity. I liked her immediately. She radiated warmth and kindness.

"Mary, I've never spoken to a psychic before. I think you're the person I've been looking for." She paused.

I could tell that she was not well. Her outward appearance was fine, although she was a bit pale and thin. It was the particular shade of green of her aura (the invisible field surrounding a person) that revealed her weakened condition to me.

"I'm quite ill," she stated without sentiment.

"It's your heart," I confirmed.

"Now I see how the gift works," she laughed.

Molly became serious and told me her story.

Essentially, she had "died" on the operating table, visited the astral plane, and returned to her body. She reported the adventure to me in vivid detail. First she heard the doctor yell at the nurse, "My God, we're losing her." Then she was above her body, looking at the staff who were trying to revive her. As she was watching her body on the table, she heard a loud noise—almost a roar—followed by fast movement. Then she felt herself moving toward a bright light and the shadow of a person in the distance.

"Were you afraid?" I asked.

"Not for a second," she told me.

Her uncle Al was the person who greeted her. It was odd for her to see him, as she had not been particularly close to him before his passing. He smiled warmly and made her feel safe. He took Molly's hand, telling her they must hurry, as they had little time.

One of her most vivid memories was that her feet and legs felt cold though the top part of her body was unaffected. Al instructed her to hold tight so she wouldn't fall, not knowing how to move in spirit. He laughed as he explained the humor of watching new souls fall down as they tried to do "the spirit walk." He had compared it to watching a Chaplin movie.

To Molly it felt like flying. They arrived in front of a large Gothic-type structure. As they went inside, Al said there was someone who wanted to speak to her. They entered what looked like a boardroom. There was an enormous table with approximately one hundred chairs. The woman sitting at the end of the table urged them to hurry.

Al moved faster. The same woman told Molly to sit

down, that there was nothing to fear. "Listen carefully to me. There's a job for you to do on the earth. When you've finished, you'll be back here with us," she told Molly firmly but kindly.

Sensing Molly's disappointment at the thought of going back to the earth, the woman chided her. "Now, don't be a baby. You agreed to this before you were born. It doesn't matter that you don't recall the agreement. It's a karmic situation."

The woman went on to explain Molly's task: She was to return to physical life and find a psychic named Mary who lived in Greenwich Village. Molly must tell her the story of her visit to the astral plane. The lady went on to explain that the psychic was writing a book about her personal experiences with viewing the other side, and Molly's story would be helpful to educate others. She told Molly that Mary would get the information across to the public. When you locate Mary, tell her that "the old lady" sends her regards. She'll know what that means. Do you have any questions?

"What is the psychic's last name? Where in the Village does she live? How will I find her?" Molly questioned.

"You're a clever girl. It is your job to find her. You can't expect to have things so easy. You'll know that she's the right person because she's the one writing the book. Al, take your niece through the gardens and then show her the way back. I'll be waiting for you when you return to this side of life. Now, go on, you have work to do." The lady waved good-bye. Molly then said to me, "I wish I could explain the beauty of the gardens. I've never seen flowers like the ones over there. They're so alive, you expect them to say hello. I understood why this place was called paradise. I could have looked at the landscape forever, but Al told me it was time to go back to my body."

"The next thing I remember is waking up in the recovery room." Molly paused and waited for me to reply.

I sensed that Molly feared that I wouldn't believe her.

"How did you find me?" I asked.

"First, I was confused when I woke up. It took me days to remember the whole incident. The doctor told me that I had had a close call. Everyone had been very worried. My sister cried, telling me that I had died and it was a miracle that I was alive. As my strength was restored, I had a great desire to tell people what I had seen. My sister didn't really believe me. I decided not to tell my parents. It didn't seem necessary." She paused.

Molly then related her search for me. Since she had never gone to a psychic before, she wasn't familiar with anyone in the profession. She called various spiritualist churches with no luck. Her friends weren't helpful. Her search ended when she picked up a magazine in her doctor's office and spotted an article about various psychics, including one Mary T. Browne who lives in Greenwich Village.

"You're writing the book, aren't you?" She held her breath, waiting for my reply.

"Yes, Molly, I am."

She then started to cry tears of relief, and I assured her that her story would be reported verbatim.

"Molly, can you tell me a bit more about 'the old lady'?" I asked.

"She was a very large woman. Her head was covered with a scarf. Her clothes looked like they were from the last century. She spoke quickly with an accent that I couldn't recognize. I was struck by the intensity of her eyes. The woman appeared to be very busy. Her presence could have been intimidating if I hadn't felt a great flow of love from her." She paused to catch her breath.

"Who is she and why does she call herself 'the old lady'?" Molly inquired.

I explained that she was a teacher of mine. Molly was correct in dating her clothes to the last century, as she passed over in 1891. It may sound disrespectful to call someone "the old lady," but in this case it's an affectionate name used only by those close to her.

"The old lady" continues her work in spirit, inspiring certain people. I've been tuned in to her for twenty years, and her influence from the other side has been a great support in my work. We're helped by those in spirit if we've earned this assistance. Often, "the old lady" comes to me directly. Everything she does has a specific point. She used Molly as a messenger to educate people about near-death experience.

Molly and I became good friends. She soaked up knowledge like a sponge. I lent her books on reincarnation and karma. I met her family. They were nice people who loved Molly very much. We didn't have to work to convince them of the reality of her journey. Deeply spiritual people themselves, they believed in their own afterlife. Many times she laughed and reminded me it was *my* job to inform people, not hers.

Molly passed over less than a year ago. I was with her at her mother's house the evening before her passing. There was little for us to say. Her last words to me were "Can I do anything over there for you?"

"Thank 'the old lady' for me. Also please find my

friend Nicky and tell him that I love him very much," I answered.

"I'd be happy to," she replied. She became quiet for a moment, then asked, "Mary, do you think I might be able to help 'the old lady'? So many times it has occurred to me to ask you. I know that many people work in the spirit world. Is it arrogant of me to think 'the old lady' might be able to use my help? I'll be leaving you shortly. I keep seeing Uncle Al when I close my eyes. He keeps saying I'll be home soon." She rested.

"Molly, you certainly can help her. You'd be a wonderful assistant. Don't forget that you're linked to 'the old lady' karmically. It was no accident that you were chosen to deliver the message to me. You have served many by your story and your personal courage. You'll continue to serve on the other side."

The next morning Molly left us to go "home."

As I promised, I have told you her story.

WORSHIP

It doesn't matter what your religious affiliation is on earth. You may pray in spirit if you so desire. On arrival into spirit, many people see that this isn't necessary. All life of service is a form of prayer. Any act of gratitude is praying.

You'll find services of all denominations taking place in spirit, and you may choose to partake or not. Some people feel better in the vibration of their earthly churches or temples.

A very large nondenominational spiritual center stands in the middle of the activity. Everyone is welcome. In the middle there stands an enormous organ.

Large stained-glass windows give the building an un-
canny beauty. It is not unusual to hear Liszt or Bach
playing for the enjoyment of all who wish to listen.
Other great teachers play to inspire the spirit folk. One
can sometimes hear the music on the earth.

MUSIC

At midnight, on Christmas Eve 1984, I was sitting in
my living room with some friends, talking, when I
heard the faint sound of music. It was unearthly and at
the same time very real. As I concentrated, a woman's
voice singing "Silent Night" flowed through my mind.
I clearly heard a "choir of angels" behind the singer. I
focused my vision into the astral world.

The singer was Madame Schumann-Heink. I recognized her face, not her voice. There was an enormous
Christmas tree lit with candles, and thousands of people
were watching the concert. I related everything to the
group in my apartment.

Since that year I have been able to tune in to the concert every Christmas Eve. The spirit world celebrates
Christmas on the day we on earth do. Though it's not
necessary for them to do this, since they live each moment in the spirit of Christmas, it's a respectful act
toward those on earth who enjoy celebrating holidays.
Of course, no one is expected to attend any service that
isn't part of his or her religious belief system. There are
services for each religion open to anyone who would
like to attend.

Talented singers who pass over still enjoy using their
voices in spirit, so at any given time there are performances going on there. Musicians are busy continuing

their work. Composers will use singers to try new
works, or to stage pieces. Orchestras that no longer
have to depend on donations thrive in spirit. Music in
spirit is more alive and fuller. The best way I can relate
the difference between music on earth and in spirit is to
compare mono and stereo.

MOZART

In 1985 and 1986 I was visited frequently by Wolfgang
Amadeus Mozart. At the time, I had a group of very talented clients who used a great deal of his music in their
projects.

During a session with one of them, I looked over at
my piano, and standing there, fully costumed in
eighteenth-century attire, was Wolfgang. It just so happened we were playing a cut from *The Magic Flute*.
Delighted, he kept telling me "that is my music."

He visited at least ten times over a two-year period.
Always, he stood in the same spot next to my piano,
appearing only when he could give input to creative
clients. They, not possessing my clairvoyant or clairau-
dient abilities, could not see or hear him. A few times
one of these clients would remark just how amazing my
musical knowledge was. If they had only known.

I learned a great deal about music and spirit from
Lawrence's teacher, Sir William. Sir William had been
a great composer of music and shared some of his
works with me. I'd visited him at his home in the country as well as at his place in the city. He talked to me
of the various "music devas" (a deva is also the word
for "angel" or "spirit") who work to inspire mankind
with music thought forms. Sir William talked at length

about the future of healing people—mentally, physically, and spiritually—with music, using specific combinations of tones. The proper combinations could directly affect the nervous system, helping to balance the total body.

He was quite distressed about the direction music had taken during this century. He felt that "too many negative thought forms have permeated the music due to the vibration of drugs entering into the musicians' auras. This has created disharmony. It's necessary to be a clear channel—clear of any substances that can fog the creative force—to write healing music. Alcohol and drugs are harmful influences to man's spiritual growth." Sir William believes that mankind will become more aware of this as time goes on. "I'm delighted that the music of some of our great friends like Mozart has been used in popular movies," he told me.

"This influence has a positive effect on the planet. It opens the minds of people to this beautiful vibration. Many wouldn't have heard this great music if it hadn't been reintroduced through the medium of the cinema," he added.

I asked him why I'd never heard rock music on the other side. I've heard only classical music and operas.

He explained that rock music can't survive in devachan because its vibration is of an earthly matter. It's not that it's bad or good; it just dissipates before it reaches the higher realms.

Everyone that I'd seen in devachan appeared perfectly happy with the choice of music. What Sir William said made a great deal of sense to me. It wasn't a matter of taste, it was a question of vibration.

Sir William

The only thing more blissful than sitting with my dear
teacher Lawrence is being in the company of both Lawrence and his teacher, Sir William.

In fall 1992, three years had passed since I'd last
been in the physical presence of Sir William. I'd often
thought about my previous meetings with this great man
who possessed an incomparable healing, comforting
warmth. I'd always felt very calm in his presence. He
appeared to be in his late sixties, but it was hard to tell
for sure. His eyes had both the sparkle of someone very
young and an incredible intensity. Lawrence showed
great respect for Sir William.

You can imagine my happiness when I received a
note inviting me to visit them in the country. A car
picked me up at the designated time, and a few hours
later we arrived at the house. I'd been there before, yet
the beauty seemed even greater than I'd remembered.
The landscaping and foliage were comparable only to
my visions of the astral.

As I stood looking at the fantastically beautiful yard,
I heard Lawrence's voice.

"Thinking about Scotland?" he asked.

I nodded, and was not surprised to hear he'd been
there too.

I told Lawrence how I'd seen the spirit of a dear
friend of mine while I was in Scotland, someone who'd
passed over shortly before I'd arrived at Findhorn. His
passing had caused me a great deal of grief. Though I
understand that no one dies, I miss my friend very
much.

John, Scotland, and the Karmic Connection

I walked alone toward the village of Findhorn one very crisp afternoon. It was misting slightly. Though I had intended to walk a straight path toward town, something made me turn off onto a side road. Feeling overcome with fatigue, I sat down next to a tree. A slight chill passed through me. Suddenly, standing in front of me, was my departed friend John. He did a little dance for me and then started laughing. John had been an actor and director while on earth. It was obvious that he'd retained his theatrical flair in spirit.

He'd passed on, shortly before my trip, in a car accident in New York. At first I felt terrible that my grief over his passing made him feel that he had to visit me.

Yes, John's passing had been a shock and I'd missed him a great deal. He had been a mentor to me. We'd met in college and had both moved to New York from Iowa at about the same time. His insights into acting had always helped me. Still, I wouldn't have intentionally pulled him back to the physical to comfort me. As I stared at John, it confused me that he would come to Scotland.

He laughed as he talked to me about his passing.

"It was an accident," he said with a tone of sarcasm.

John then went on to explain how his thinking had changed once he'd reached the other side.

"There are no accidents in a perfectly ordered universe run by universal law," he explained. "It was my time to go forward, so the car crashed. It's really quite simple. People make it more complicated than it is." Again he laughed.

Then he told me to stop feeling guilty that he'd come to visit me. "I had little trouble clearing when I arrived into spirit. You were always talking about the astral plane and spirit life. You thought that I didn't take you seriously, but I did. It was my nature to make jokes about things that I didn't understand. It must have seemed like I was making fun of your beliefs. I'm sorry if I hurt your feelings," he told me.

I assured him he hadn't hurt me.

He continued his story.

On arrival into spirit he had explored for a while, overwhelmed by the beauty and the activity of this world. He met his grandmother and a few other friends who had gone on before him. John had painted as a hobby and was a great lover of art. He spoke of the colors and vibrancy of the artworks and of his surprise at the magnitude of the galleries. He very excitedly reported seeing well-known actors and playwrights whose works he had greatly admired.

John then reported his encounter with a Native American who had approached him and informed him that they had a mutual friend on earth—me.

"We talked about you for a few minutes and then he told me that there was something I needed to do," John said.

White Feather explained to John that he should visit me in Scotland. He hadn't told John the exact reason. He just told John to visit me.

One of my most vivid recollections of this meeting with John was that he seemed blissful. While on the earth John had often seemed sad—not negative, but dispirited. All vibrations of gloom had dissipated. He radiated happiness.

I thanked him for delivering this message. I felt no need to burden him with details of earthly life. As he faded from my sight, tears streamed down my cheeks. These were tears of reverence and gratitude. John had found the peace of mind he'd been seeking. And I'd been given a remarkable gift.

Lawrence broke the spell of my story by touching my shoulder.

"Now the trip to Scotland makes a great deal of sense. The meeting with John was a tremendous privilege. John earned the right to be the messenger. It occurred in Scotland because you and John lived a past life together in that country. Also, it's a very psychic environment," Lawrence explained.

The moment I arrived in Scotland it was clear to me that I'd been there before. Though it was cold and rainy, I felt terrific. Findhorn interested me a great deal, but it was the country that captivated me. I asked Lawrence to explain my past-life relationship with John.

"John was your sister. The two of you lived very near the place where John appeared to you. When you first met John at school, did he seem familiar?" Lawrence asked.

"John was much older than I was. When I was a freshman he was a third-year grad student. We first met in the costume shop, where he was designing the wardrobe for a play, intimidating everyone with his caustic wit. He barked an order at me and I told him off. He stared at me and then started laughing. From that day on he was my best friend at school. I guess he was a bit like a sister to me in this life as well. He had a good combination of male and female energy. We could talk for hours about everything. He was one of the few people in college whom I discussed metaphysics with, and I always felt totally comfortable with him," I replied.

BLISS

After this lesson Lawrence took me to meet Sir William.

The Tudor-style mansion was just as I remembered it. Lawrence showed me to the library. Sir William sat in a wing chair with his dog next to his feet.

"Come here, my child, and let's have a look at you," Sir William said with great warmth.

"The last time you were here I was away on business. I heard that Lawrence took you on a hike. How do you like our pleasant home?" He took my hand and nodded toward the chair beside him.

I sat down and then answered, "This is my idea of devachan."

The two gentlemen laughed.

"Well, you'll be too busy working in devachan to have much time to enjoy sitting in a house," Sir William answered.

"That's fine with me. I'll be happy to do anything that I can," I assured them.

The door opened and tea was brought in for us. Lawrence poured and then the three of us sat quietly for a few minutes. As we sat enjoying the silence, I recalled the last time we were together.

"The silence is where the spirit dwells," Sir William had said that day.

The silence of that moment had a beautiful vibration. It was the quiet one feels in a church or temple.

The wind howled and the dog sat up.

Lawrence told Sir William my Scotland story.

"A mystical place indeed. I've always enjoyed my times there immensely. After we finish our tea I would like to show you my greenhouse." He looked at me.

"I'd love to see it." I smiled.

When we'd finished, Sir William told Lawrence that we needed a few moments alone. Lawrence appeared very pleased and said he'd see us a little later. Sir William and I went outside.

The mountains stood behind the house with great dignity. As we walked, Sir William pointed out various types of trees and bushes. There were beautiful peach roses in bloom, the same kind Lawrence had left for me on Martha's Vineyard. The grounds were very expansive, every inch perfectly landscaped. Arriving at the greenhouse, we entered and walked through. Sir William had an amazing array of herbs. He explained the healing qualities of many of them.

"Our gardeners in the spirit world are looking into the various herbs and their medicinal qualities. We on earth are aware of very few herbs. In time, when man is more open-minded, he will see that every ill can be healed through natural substances. For the time being, the doctors will continue to write prescriptions for their various pills. The Egyptians knew a great deal about healing. Tragically, most of their records were lost when the Alexandrian libraries burned. Humanity has never recovered from the loss of that body of knowledge." He paused.

"Doesn't everything exist in the spirit world?" I asked.

"Yes, my dear, but mankind must rediscover the lost

knowledge while in the physical body. We can't interfere with individual karma. Our friends in spirit have
time to examine qualities of known herbs. They must
reincarnate into the physical in order to further pursue
knowledge. Few souls have reached a level where they
can understand certain books. Knowledge can be dangerous if placed in the hands of those not prepared for
it. That's why a great deal of knowledge was lost to
mankind. You're well aware that there are many realms
in the spirit world. Certain libraries of learning are in
the higher realms, available only to a few worthy of
embracing these great treasures of knowledge." He
stopped speaking and studied me.

"Let's sit here for a moment." He motioned me toward
a bench.

We sat together on the bench that looked like a
church pew. Light streamed in through the beautiful
glass walls and ceiling. In the corner to the right of the
bench was a magnificent stained-glass window. Peace
permeated the atmosphere. For a moment I felt as if I
were no longer in my physical body. The light coming
into the room became much brighter. The plants took on
a deep intensity. A passionate energy enveloped my total being, and I felt more alive than I'd ever been. This
was total bliss. Thoughts of love and compassion for all
life rushed through my head. I then became aware of
Sir William gazing at me. He pressed my hand while he
smiled with loving understanding.

SIR WILLIAM SPEAKS OF HEAVEN

"Think of a moment when you were in a total state of
peace of mind. This is heaven.

"All worry has been removed. Fear can't survive in this environment. Harmony reigns in all life here. Evil has no home, for it can breathe only in an aura of disharmony. Physical matter doesn't exist on this plane, so there can be no decay.

"The horizons are endless, the realms infinite. You live in your own perfect dream-state. You arrive into your spirit home as you left your earthly one. You maintain your personality and your individuality.

"Physical life is the place to work on our character. Heaven allows us a rest from our world-weary physical bodies. It allows us time to recharge our spirit parts in order to continue our journey toward pure harmony.

"You'll be with those whom you loved on earth. You'll experience whatever your ego is drawn toward. As you grow into spiritual maturity, your view of heavenly peace matures. At this level the realms of the spirit become purer, the colors fuller, the sounds more finely tuned.

"Life doesn't end. It continues and becomes more alive."

He stopped speaking. The silence was interrupted by the sound of organ music. We sat together for a few more minutes, then he rose from the bench, took my arm, and escorted me to the house.

Lawrence was waiting for us in the library, and I knew that he was aware of my mystical experience. For those few minutes sitting next to Sir William, I'd felt totally at one with all life.

"You must remember that feeling, my child. Keep it close to your heart and it will support you throughout your daily life," Lawrence said with great feeling. "You experienced total bliss. This is the same feeling that the soul will experience as it reaches the other side. It's rare to explore this feeling while still in the physical body." He paused and looked over at Sir William.

Sir William was once again sitting in front of the fire, meditating.

Sir William finally spoke. "It's unfortunate for people that they live in a constant state of fear. Understanding that life continues after the physical ceases is the greatest tonic against fear."

Lawrence walked me to the car. He pressed my hand and told me that he'd be in touch soon. There was no need for more words between us. The drive back to the city seemed to take only minutes. I arrived home feeling very centered. A profound feeling of the sacredness of all life enveloped me. We can find heaven on earth. It is right in front of us. It lives within our hearts. We just need to love each other. It really is quite simple.

✳ 4

Hell

Almost everyone on earth right now will experience one of the heavenly realms I described when they pass over. But there is another place—where only the most utterly depraved, remorseless, evil people will go when they die. We will call this place hell.

Hell is the Land of No Shapes. It is completely dark and nothing can grow. No good feelings are allowed. There is no kindness, no friendship, and no love. There is only the torment of your own mistakes. Some souls do eventually get out, but others never do. Hell's the worst punishment imaginable.

But rest assured only the worst actions, followed by *no remorse*, will place a soul into these realms. A person must be wicked beyond imagination to reside there. Normal human frailties are not the food for hell.

Each soul that lands there has damned itself into the region. We are given many chances for redemption. But some just refuse to repent, therefore they remain in hell for eternity and do not reincarnate.

The inhabitants are shapeless—total distortions of their former selves. Words to describe this place—abyss, Hades, Satan's home, or the place of the damned—do it no justice.

What I'm describing isn't pleasant, but I'm not trying to frighten people, merely to inform them of the existence of this area of the spirit world. I know no person inhabiting this realm, nor have I received communication from a soul residing there, so I'll tell you how I came upon this information.

The Trip to Hell

It was with great trepidation that I'd asked Lawrence to show me the dark realms of the spirit world. I had never wanted to see the dark side. I knew it existed. That was enough for me. But I felt it necessary to experience both sides of the astral plane in order better to comprehend the complexity of the afterlife.

One evening Lawrence came to my apartment. It was unusual but not surprising that he called and inquired if he might come over, then arrived moments later. Dressed in khakis and a blue blazer with a white shirt, he could have been a regular guy walking down the street. It never failed to amaze me just how normal Lawrence seemed. It was obvious after spending time in his company that he was special. Still, he managed to fit in wherever he went. There were no robes or garments that set him apart. It was the feeling I had in his presence that confirmed his greatness of soul.

As I made a pot of tea, I filled him in on the events in my life. He was always interested in every little aspect of my world. He asked questions about my friends and my work. I poured him a cup of tea and we sat down and continued our chat.

Lawrence related greetings from Sir William and we talked about a future trip to the country house. I was eager to return as soon as possible. After a short while the light conversation changed to a serious tone.

"I've been concerned, as you seem overwhelmed by your workload," he said.

"I'm okay, Lawrence, a bit shell-shocked about an incident that occurred yesterday. A client frightened me. He acted quite unbalanced. I felt a negative influence around him that appeared to be in control of his personality. It's rare for me to feel fear during a session. He was referred by a friend, so I wasn't apprehensive about seeing him."

"How did you handle this?" he asked.

"I sent very strong thoughts in your direction. It appears to have worked." We laughed.

"No matter what I said to this man, he snapped at me. His negativity was making it impossible to help him. After ten minutes of this battle I used shock treatment." I sighed and then continued.

"I banged the arm of the chair and told the influence to get out of my house. The influence was childish and nasty, not demonic. It was a little spirit that attached itself to his astral body. This spirit acted like an obnoxious child, arguing for no reason. This action stunned my client, and the elemental left him. The man grew calmer and started to cry. He'd no idea that his overindulgence in alcohol opened him to attract astral beings floating about in the air. He'd been drinking before he'd arrived, which made him act in a way contrary to his true character. When I looked at him I saw a good man in torment. He realized he had a serious drinking problem, but felt unable to stop. He was terrified he'd go to hell if he didn't stop drinking."

"I explained that everyone has something in life to overcome. The process can seem like hell because it's often difficult to conquer."

"He's living in the hell of his addiction. It takes time and understanding to overcome this. It can take more than one life to overcome a specific problem. This poor man is confusing hellish for hell," Lawrence commented.

"Lawrence, I've seen many images of devachan, of heaven. The realms are beautiful. I know the dark realms known as hell exist even though I've not seen them. It's not a desire to see hell, but a need to know the facts. I think I should experience both sides of the afterlife. White Feather has never focused my clairvoyance toward the lower levels. Would you help me to see what they're like?" I waited for a reply.

He thought for quite a while before he answered.

"It makes perfect sense that you've not been exposed to the lower realms of negativity. First of all, no one you know has ever gone there. It's *extremely* rare that a soul goes to these realms. Some people go to less blissful realms than others. Only the completely depraved go to those lower realms." He paused.

After reflecting, he said it appeared necessary for me to take a little trip. I must not be afraid. I'd be protected.

He pointed to a specific corner of the room and instructed me to focus all my energy on that spot. I concentrated intensely. As I gazed into the corner, the smell of smoke entered the room. Lawrence warned me not to lose my concentration. He informed me that the smell was not physical, but part of the vibration from the dark realm.

The screen came into my vision and I saw the dark, shapeless picture I described earlier. It was horrible. The absence of even a drop of kindness or love was shattering. Lawrence warned me again to show no fear. I must admit I would have been terrified if Lawrence hadn't been with me. The veil between worlds is very thin, and I had no desire to get any closer to this evil area.

The vision lasted only a minute, long enough for me to look upon this wickedness. The picture faded and a cold chill went through the room. I felt as though I might vomit. My whole body was weak. The smell of smoke hung in the air.

It took a few minutes to regain my composure. Lawrence got up and poured some tea into my cup. His strong, serene presence gave me comfort.

"You've seen the worst, my child. Your sensitive nature will need time to recover." He seemed concerned.

"Please don't worry, Lawrence. I asked you to help me. One must have the courage to accept the reality, no matter how terrible it is."

The place known as hell did exist. I'd seen it. Souls there were in great torment. The darkness was almost impenetrable.

"My child, every soul is given many chances to get out of this area. They arrived there by their own hand. No person is damned by anyone but himself. The law of retribution [another name for karma] is quite clear on this. No person goes anywhere he's not attracted by his own actions."

Lawrence stayed with me another hour. He explained

hell in depth. The worst criminals inhabit this dark area, the soulless. Even the tiniest glimmer of remorse frees a soul from this self-damnation.

He left that evening with the promise to contact me soon. I went to sleep grateful to be in my lovely bed. I released the images of the lowest realms. I knew that they existed and I had to acknowledge that. But it was important not to dwell on hell, as it involved very few souls. It's much better to concentrate one's energy on what helps the most people.

I want to reiterate that almost nobody goes to hell when they pass over. Most of us are rewarded in spirit by going to the blissful realms in heaven. On earth we face challenges, overcome fears, and grow wiser.

Hell is a very real place, where the truly evil spirits suffer for their sins. But the other side is not usually a place of suffering.

Unfortunately, many of us create our own hell on earth—in the physical—attracting torment by our past mistakes. This is completely unnecessary, but all too common.

Don

For some people, going to hell is their greatest fear. It was terrifying Don as he lay dying. He wouldn't be comforted by his friends or family. His brother asked me to visit, knowing I'd had experience helping people pass over. His mother sat by his bed with tears running down her cheeks. She looked at me as I entered, her eyes imploring me to help. The aura in the room was heavy and dark. The first thing I did was open the window, letting light and air pour in.

"Don't open that," Don snapped.

I walked up to him and said firmly, "Don, stop it. Your mother needs some air."

This stunned him into silence. I motioned to his mother to leave us alone. I took a deep breath and asked him why he thought he'd go to hell. He talked nonstop for a few minutes. He'd convinced himself that he was bound for hell because he'd stopped attending church services a few years earlier.

Don was a very fine person who'd lived with dignity and compassion. He was loved by everyone who knew him. It was tragic to hear him talk like this. Cancer had invaded his body and, unfortunately, had been detected only at a late stage. Not one to neglect his body, this situation was karmic for Don. It was simply his time to go on. There was nothing whatsoever about his life that was evil.

What kind of God did Don believe in? What doctrine taught that good people lived in hell for not attending church services?

We talked for a long time, and I shared my experiences with the other side. He listened with deep interest, yet I felt I wasn't reaching him. I paused for a moment and said a quiet prayer, asking for help. Often in moments of deep concern I ask the God Force to give me guidance. Some call the God Force God, or Lord. I speak of the higher consciousness that lives within each one of us as the God Force. I wasn't certain how to best help Don.

At approximately five o'clock Don received a special message. I'd glanced at my watch while the nurse came in to give him some medication. She left us and I felt cold and a bit spaced-out. I looked toward the window, and a clear image of a man in a fishing boat came into my psychic view. The window became a screen for me. The man was quite thin, dressed in a plaid flannel shirt and jeans. He was waving a red cap. I then heard him say, "Tell Don that Pop says it's suppertime."

I gave the message to Don. He appeared stunned and asked me to describe the person in my mind's eye. He was especially interested in the cap. As I described the man, the vision slowly began to fade.

Don remained quiet for a few moments. He very calmly explained who this man was. Pop was the name he called his grandfather who had passed over ten years before. Don had loved fishing with his "Pop." He'd given Pop the red cap for a birthday gift and Pop always wore it when they went fishing. Every time they were together, at five o'clock Pop would take off his cap and tell Don, "Hurry now, it's time for supper. We mustn't be late, or your grandma will be angry with us."

I waited a few minutes and then asked, "Don, do you think that your grandpa was a good man?"

"The best!" he answered.

"Did he go to church every week?" I questioned.

"No, as a matter of fact, he didn't."

"That's interesting. He sure looked happy to me, Don. He wanted you to know that he's fine, and that you'll be fine with him."

Don smiled for the first time since I'd arrived. Then he laughed out loud. His mother entered the room as he lay there, chuckling. She looked at me with puzzlement.

"What's going on?"

I told her to ask Don, that I had to go. Then I left the room with deep gratitude for the spirit help that I'd received.

I was positive that Don's fears wouldn't return. Pop would be waiting for him at the border, assuring him that he was arriving into a heavenly place.

Don's fear is perfectly normal. I've encountered many people who think that their human flaws will damn them. This fantasy stems from misinformation or indoctrination.

I know dozens of people who go to church regularly—"just in case" they're damned for not attending. Many of these people don't believe in the doctrine, much less find peace in church.

Not everyone who fears hell will receive a comforting message from the other side. Don had earned the right to hear from his dear grandfather. Some people release fear by reading about the experience of people like Don. Others find out as soon as they pass over that their fears were unfounded.

Just remember that hell on earth can be living a life with the fear of damnation. By eliminating that fear, we can live happier, more productive lives.

The Woman on the Highway

In August 1984 I was traveling from Albuquerque to Santa Fe. It was dark and there were few cars on the road. My friend Tim, who was quite in tune with my psychic gifts, drove the car. The highway has many curves, and it spirals upward as you drive toward Santa Fe. We were chatting as we drove, having a nice, calm trip. At one point we took a curve, and as we turned, the headlights beamed onto the side of the road, where I saw a woman crawling along the highway.

"Pull off the road. There's a woman who needs help," I told Tim.

"I didn't see anyone," he replied.

"She's in spirit," I told him.

He quickly pulled off the road and found a flashlight for me. I got out and backtracked, using the flashlight to guide me to the woman.

I found her easily. It took a moment before I was able to communicate with her. She told me there had been a car crash and she couldn't find her child. She was hysterical. She had no idea she was dead. I'm sure the accident had been a shock and there had been no time to register her death.

I didn't know if the baby was on this side or on the other one. I knew I'd have to try to get her to let go of the physical.

She could remain in this state between worlds indefinitely if someone didn't help her. Tim joined me and observed. He'd known me for a good many years and had seen my work. Nothing fazed him, and he wanted to be supportive.

I talked to her for at least an hour. I asked the spirit guides to assist in her transition. (I'd had little experience with this type of situation and I needed all the help I could get.) It wasn't clear how long she had been in that condition. A skirt and blouse was her classic outfit. I couldn't tell from her clothing when the accident had occurred. I repeated over and over that her baby was fine and that she must pass over in order to see the child again. (This was true whether the child was of the earth or in spirit.)

I got down and crawled with her, trying to gain her confidence. I think the helpers from the other side inspired her to listen closely to me. I was beginning to think I wouldn't be able to convince her to go over, when suddenly she vanished. I knew the transition had been made.

I was relieved. It's terrible to be caught between two worlds. Shock is the major cause of this condition, and this woman wasn't the only soul in this state. Battlefields are overrun with marching soldiers not aware they've been shot. They keep marching until they are convinced to go to the spirit world.

These poor souls had no time to prepare for death. The mind didn't register the death, so the astral body remained earthbound. There are special spirit helpers in charge of talking to these poor souls. Often, it takes many years to convince someone that they must leave the earth. The helpers never give up, and eventually the soul is able to make the transition.

Haunted houses are inhabited by those who can't or won't go over to the other side because of a shocking death, an overattachment to the physical, or, at the worst, a vendetta. Not all haunting spirits are evil. Many are just confused. It depends on the reason the soul is earthbound.

Fortunately, I could help this dear lady; her karma brought a psychic to that particular road. I've returned to that part of the country many times, and every time I'm on the highway, I check to make certain that she's gone.

Being stuck between two worlds is not hell. It's simply a state of consciousness attracted by certain souls who have difficulty making the transition from earth to spirit. The best explanation of hell lies in the understanding of the law of retribution. There is absolute justice. We attract what we've earned. This applies to the spirit realms as well as to the earth plane.

The baby born blind has done nothing in this life to attract that situation. It's a challenge for the soul. The only rational explanation for this seeming injustice lies in reincarnation, where the test is attributed to experiences in a past life or lives.

A good man may reside next to an evil one in order to inspire the evildoer toward goodness. We must balance all our actions while living in our physical bodies. *No evil act goes unpunished. Nor does a good action go unrewarded.* The choice lies within the individual.

Overcoming Fear

Little children hide under their bedcovers, shaking with fear that their white lie will place them in the halls of Satan. This is a tragic misconception. They must be taught right from wrong, but fear isn't a healthy instructor.

History changes the requirements for entry into hell. At various points in time, eating meat on Friday, going hatless into church, or getting divorced (no matter what the reason) were tickets into the realms of hell.

As social mores change, the requirements for damnation change.

A dear client of mine thought it was a sin to fly on the Sabbath. It turned out that it really upset his mother.

I didn't want to be disrespectful to his mother or to his faith, and I told him it was wrong to do anything that went against his belief system. We all have to live with ourselves.

I felt sorry for him. He was confused and really didn't know what he believed. He'd been told since he was a child that something was sinful and this now caused him to live in torment. It was truly a reaction to indoctrination, but he'd have to come to terms with his own belief system. Questioning rules of conduct that made no sense to him was a test for his own soul development. He mustn't be motivated by fear. This type of motivation can cause depression and anger.

Religion is an individual choice. We don't have to belong to a certain religion in order to find enlightenment. The God Force lives within each one of us and doesn't damn us for flying on Friday or for going hatless in church.

The soul incarnates into a specific religion for karmic reasons in order to help fulfill its destiny. We've no right to impose our own beliefs on others. Formal religious training isn't a requirement for redemption. It's a grand goal to live a good, useful life of service—a goal that can be achieved within or outside of structured religion.

In spirit there's no such thing as religious prejudice or persecution. This type of behavior is limited to the physical world. The greatest form of worship is found in respecting all life and living with integrity. In this way we pay homage to the God that lives within everyone.

We damn ourselves into troubled situations by our own behavior. Fearful living is a form of hell we create for ourselves on the earth plane. Love and understanding will free us from the bondage of this state of mind.

Freed from the fear of eternal damnation and similar abstract threats, we're able to discover what our true beliefs are rather than blindly adhering to doctrine we don't fully understand. We can then discover our own absolute goodness and live richer, more fulfilled lives.

Evil

Evil people do exist. It's frightening but true. But there are degrees of evil. Actions of an evil nature performed with no remorse are the most hideous.

Evil is thought of by many as a disease. The psychological history of the evil-acting person will generally show childhood trauma or abuse. This is unfortunate, but it doesn't excuse evil behavior. An evil action directed toward another will come back to the evildoer, be it during this life or the next one.

Being cruel or thoughtless may merely be mean, not evil. If we act with vicious malicious intent to cause harm, we're moving into evil territory.

The most potent strategy for overcoming evil is through evoking love.

The Need for Sensation

The need for sensation can have evil results.

If you pass over with a powerful addiction, the only way to get the sensation of the substance is by possessing someone in the physical. The soul lacking a physical body to satisfy cravings must possess one. It's necessary to be in the aura of a person who is indulging in your desired substance in order to partake. No one can be possessed unless they open themselves up to possession by specifically indulging in these substances.

POSSESSION OF A DRUNKEN MAN

I was with some friends in a nightclub one evening, and a man seated next to us was drinking quite heavily. I looked at him and saw an evil influence hovering over him, a shadow (a ghostlike being) very close to his head. The man kept ordering more drinks, and drinking them quickly, until eventually his behavior became rowdy.

I evoked the higher beings, for spiritual protection by saying a silent prayer. The dark spirit was too close for comfort.

Just as I was going to tell the man he'd better stop drinking, I saw this "spirit" enter him. It was too late and too dangerous to interfere. The most I could do was to find someone to take this fellow home. I told my friends that we should leave. They saw that I was upset, so they got ready to go. I informed the maître d' that the gentleman had had a lot to drink and needed help getting home. The maître d' knew the customer and arranged for a car to take him immediately. We left. I had no desire to wrestle with the negative vibration that possessed this gentleman. First of all, he didn't know me so it was doubtful he'd listen to anything I'd say. Secondly, the influence that entered him wouldn't tolerate my interference. Any try at reasoning with him would at that moment be in vain. When he'd sobered up, it might be possible to reason with him.

I was comforted knowing he'd been escorted home. The "influence" would leave once the drinking stopped.

We mustn't assume that the man who was possessed was evil. He was unfortunate. His overindulgence opened him up to the influence of this spirit's need to drink through him. The spirit was hovering around this bar, just waiting for someone to drink too much. I'm sure that the spirit used to frequent the place while on earth and that's why he chose to return there. His only chance to feel the sensation of the alcohol was to attach himself to the astral body of someone who overindulged.

The incident in the nightclub was upsetting though not uncommon. This was a lovely club, nothing sordid about it. The spirit was *so* addicted, he couldn't clear the physical and rest in peace. Having not overcome his addiction during his lifetime, the spirit had an unearthly need for the substance. This tragic addiction creates a desire so strong that not even death can break the bond. Only time and help from counselors in spirit can dissolve the need to hover around the earth. The spirit must reincarnate with the addiction, and he'll have another chance to overcome the addiction in the physical world.

This form of possession happens only in the most extreme forms of addiction. Certainly not every person who leaves the earth with a substance dependency will be earthbound. As they reach the spirit world, many find they've left the intensity of their desire behind with the shell of their body.

It's important to understand that addiction of any kind is a challenge we must work to overcome during the physical, or we'll be reborn with the problem as often as it takes to resolve it. Bad karma is created by addiction. It isn't unusual to hurt someone by our lack of control. Once an addiction is broken, new good karma is created.

Lawrence explained this to me. "You're protected by your own goodness. Evil influences can't get near you if you don't allow them an opening.

"Anything that removes your spiritual protection can be an opening. Excessive alcohol, drug abuse, angry, jealous thoughts, and unbalanced desires are a few examples of things that can put you in danger of being open to negative influences. And you're in no way safe from negative influences because you are ignorant of them."

This isn't a warning to make us paranoid—just aware. We must remain in control so that we won't be controlled.

Addiction isn't necessarily evil behavior and won't damn a soul into hell. It may make the transition into spirit more difficult because the soul is overly attached to the physical world, the world where these substances live.

Similarly, being possessed because we've lost control of our desires—or opened ourselves up to evil forces— doesn't doom us. It just makes life terribly unpleasant.

Being in control of strictly negative impulses—and this doesn't mean an evening cocktail, a healthy sex life, or even an occasional cigarette—but keeping balance in our earth lives will make our time in the physical and spirit more rewarding.

Again, the veil between the earth and the spirit is very thin. Spirits unable to break the attachment to the physical world hover around. Though unseen to the majority, they are close by. Spiritual strength is a great protection against unwelcome influences.

The force of evil cannot survive the power of the force of good.

"True love casts out fear."

Mystery

It's important to understand the dangers involved in dabbling with psychic forces. There are mysteries that can lead the uneducated into a world of madness.

Psychic toys such as ouija boards, automatic writing, tarot cards, or chanting mantras can ruin lives. Playing with these unseen forces can lead to insanity. These toys can be tools for conjuring up undeveloped or demonic spirits. These spirits reside close to the earth and can attach themselves to the aura of the dabbler.

Communication between earth and spirit is real. Wise people will accept this but not be driven by it. Addiction to metaphysical practices shows an inability to cope with physical life, and it's a dangerous type of escapism.

Ignorance of the danger will not shield you from it.

Dawn

Dawn was a lovely blond girl of twenty-three. She had a beautiful singing voice and dreamed of a career in music. Inquisitive by nature, she took an interest in many things, including tarot card reading. She bought a book, and began spending just a short time each day on this interest, until gradually an obsession built.

Dawn had had no experience with psychic phenomena, and perceived her interest in the tarot as fun. She had no idea of the potential danger.

I met her in the initial stages of her fascination. I warned her: "To court the psychic is to court disaster if you're not educated in all aspects of this phenomena."

But she didn't comprehend a word of my warning.

"It's just for fun. My friends and I have a glass of wine and then I do readings. They tell me that I'm really good."

"Dawn, don't tell me you're drinking wine and doing readings! Do you want to go insane? That's dangerous. There are subtle forces that you can't see waiting to possess someone as naive as you. The first rule of psychic work is *you don't mix alcohol with the gift.* Why do you think that another name for alcohol is *spirits*? It's because alcohol attracts them."

I was shaken. Her lack of knowledge frightened me. She was a good person with a fine character, yet I could see potential danger. Something she perceived as a harmless hobby was a tragedy waiting to happen. The session ended and she promised to think about my warnings.

I'm certain she thought I was overreacting. Time would teach her well.

Six months later a friend of hers, Ray, came for a session. I asked him about Dawn.

"Haven't you heard?" he asked.

"Heard what?"

"She went crazy. She started talking in different voices. It was scary. I'd be having a normal conversation with her and in the middle she'd become another person. I didn't know what to do; none of her friends did. We called her parents and they took her home. She's seeing a shrink and is on medication. Poor kid! She seemed perfectly normal when I met her. She got to the point where all she did was play with those cards and drink wine.

"I don't know for sure, but I think those cards had something to do with this. It was after she started with them that she started acting crazy," Ray told me.

I felt very sad for Dawn but relieved she was at home receiving psychological help. This is one example of the dangers of experimenting with the mysterious psychic world. Many more could be cited. The bottom line is *don't play with forces that you've not been trained to handle*!

Physical life gives us the schoolroom to balance our actions. The life we live is a composite of this one and past ones. Any situation that presents itself has been created by ourselves.

Heaven and hell are earned, not predestined. Good and evil are choices. A life of service is a great tonic for the fear of punishment.

And once again, only those souls who perform truly evil actions followed by no remorse of any kind will enter the lowest realms of spirit.

The rest of us will attract earth lives with moments of suffering and moments of joy. We will experience happiness and sorrow. And in time, with a great deal of effort, balance will reign.

It's all part of the great mystery known as life.

✳ 5

Suicide

Suicide is tragic for both the victim and the survivor. Often, it is enacted in a moment of unbearable emotional distress or total hopelessness. For some it appears to be the only way out of their torment. Loved ones left behind suffer intense grief as well as guilt—and shock at the unnatural interruption of life.

Newspapers are full of stories about people from all walks of life who choose suicide thinking it will be an end to their pain. There's even a best-selling book detailing specific methods for committing suicide. Sadly, this phenomenon isn't limited to adults: Now an alarming number of teenagers are taking their lives as well. It's as if suicide has become so commonplace that it's an acceptable alternative to dealing with life's challenges.

But suicide is *not* acceptable: It is an act of rage against the soul. Someone who takes their physical life neither lives nor dies; instead, the spirit resides between the earth and the spirit worlds until the time of its normal passing (the time that the body would have passed over if death hadn't been self-inflicted). This state—not really dead or alive—is a terrible condition of existence.

Ultimately you don't escape any hardship by ending

your life. It's not possible to kill yourself *because nobody dies.* We merely change form. People reincarnate in a future life with the same problems that drove them to suicide. It's wiser to fight through the trouble during your lifetime than to be forced to repeat it in a future life.

The body is a sacred trust. Nobody has the right to end his or her life prematurely. Tragic as it is, suicide is also a cowardly act. No one wants to suffer physical or emotional pain, depression, despair, incurable diseases, financial ruin, or the like. Many people believe they should have the right to end their lives if they're suffering, or if their quality of life has dramatically changed. I cannot stress strongly enough that you *don't* escape any hardship by ending your life.

Stella

A seriously ill woman I know was tortured by physical pain. Unable to think rationally, she swallowed a toxic amount of painkillers. Discovered a short time later by her daughter, she was eventually revived and later described to me the place she'd been while she lost consciousness.

"It was very dim, almost total darkness. The realization that I'd done something terrible to myself was awful and I wanted to get back to my body. It felt as if I were in limbo, not here or there. I could hear my daughter crying but I couldn't get back to her. It seemed impossible to go forward or backward. I prayed, begging God to let me go back to my body. I told God that when I took the pills I didn't know what I was doing. Imagine sitting in an empty, almost black space, not dead or alive, yet aware that you've hurt people. I could hear them grieving."

Stella, the client who related this story to me, is still in physical pain, but she's freed of spiritual torment. The relief of having another chance to live shines within her.

Stella is a remarkable lady with great integrity, and her act of desperation was understandable. We can't judge the power of pain. We've all experienced what seems like intolerable pain at some point. It's hard to imagine living in constant unbearable pain as Stella did. Any rational person would want to end this type of suffering. We put horses and our beloved pets out of their misery. So why should humans have to endure suffering?

Stella's story illustrates one of the negative results of suicide. The void created by suicide is far more painful than the physical pain, and spiritual suffering lives on.

Physical pain tests us in many ways. It gives us the opportunity to reach toward our higher selves and look toward the spirit, and it releases karma from past lives. (Animals don't possess the ability to reason, so they don't create karma. That's why we don't allow them to suffer.)

The person who commits suicide doesn't go to hell. As we discussed earlier, this region is reserved for the evil. It's rare that a person who commits suicide is evil: He is desperate, unbalanced, or cowardly. Evil people have no remorse for their actions, while those who kill themselves are usually very sorry immediately.

When someone does commit suicide, the soul is still attached to the physical world, but it can't be seen. In this state of limbo, the soul is aware of the pain it has caused to him- or herself and to others. It's like living in a terrible dream-state. Death for one who passes over by natural causes has been compared to sleeping a very peaceful sleep. A suicide has a very restless, tormented sleep.

Despair wears many faces. It makes people desperate or irrational. A lifetime of good actions isn't negated by one act of despair. People aren't damned for committing suicide, but they do suffer greatly. Aware that death doesn't exist, aware that you've broken a universal law, you'll also realize there is karma that must be paid. Stella's experience shows us the misery of suicide.

We've read wonderful accounts of near-death experiences. I've yet to read or hear about an account of the joy experienced in the case of a near-death by your own hand. Anyone who has attempted suicide and failed will tell you the place they went to was very unpleasant.

When it's time to reincarnate, you'll be reborn into the same situation that drove you to end your life a lifetime earlier. It will be necessary to overcome this challenge without terminating the physical experiences. Suicide merely delays physical problems and triggers new spiritual ones.

Is It Ever Acceptable to End Our Lives?

To take your life in order to protect a higher truth is an act of courage and selflessness, an act that is divinely protected.

For example: A resistance fighter is captured and he holds a secret that could save or forfeit hundreds of lives. It's certain his captors will torture him to force him to release the information. He chooses death over betrayal. He protects the higher ideal. Through this act of courage, freedom is protected and many lives are saved. This action isn't punished, it's revered. The motivation is highly spiritual.

Japanese kamikaze pilots stayed in their planes to insure they'd hit their target, even knowing death was certain. Their motive was to protect their country. Again this situation isn't looked upon as suicide, because the motive is to protect a higher ideal.

Only in cases of *selfless* behavior motivated by the highest ideals is suicide acceptable. It's not acceptable to commit this act in order to escape life's problems.

Joan

Joan overdosed on drugs "accidentally," she said. I visited her at the hospital. She looked frightened and sad when we talked about her near-death experience.

"I can't recall everything. I just remember the desperate feeling of wanting to get back to my body. I was in a dark, cold, lonely place."

Joan admitted she'd been depressed and angry prior to taking too many tranquilizers, but swore she didn't overdose on purpose.

Joan's boyfriend had left her and she wasn't happy in her job. She'd always thought she'd wind up marrying her ex and hadn't been able to cope with his decision to call it quits. Despair had set in. Always one to take her "calming pills," as she called them, this time she overdid it. She believed her overdose was an accident. But who knows what was going on in her subconscious? Joan was given a second chance, and she was grateful.

"There've been many times in the last few months when I've felt like dying. Now I'm grateful to be alive."

The last time I saw Joan she was beaming with happiness. She had a new job and a new beau. She was volunteering two nights a week at a teen center. Her near-death was the beginning of a new life.

Rosa

A client named Rosa arrived for a session looking despondent. She was bone-thin and couldn't stop crying. I handed her a tissue and listened. She wasn't interested in predictions, she wanted only comfort.

"I just want to kill myself," she kept repeating.

I was alarmed because I could tell that she meant this.

Rosa talked for the next hour. Her husband had been seeing another woman but insisted he didn't want a divorce. She hadn't been able to get angry at him; instead, she lived for his phone calls and visits.

"I'm nothing. He tells me I'm stupid and useless," she said.

I immediately told her she needed therapy. This situation required a psychiatrist, not a psychic.

Rosa's mother came from Spain to stay with her. Rosa didn't need to be alone. I called a close friend of Rosa's right after she left and told her of my deep concern. Her friend promised to keep an eye on Rosa, and to call a doctor if necessary.

Two months later Rosa returned looking much better. She'd met a new love and no longer felt the urge to end her life. I was relieved that the crisis had passed, yet saddened and worried by her thinking. It would be necessary for Rosa to find a deeper purpose to her life, or it was likely that she'd slip back into despair again. Any kind of heartbreak could set her off.

We all want to be loved and respected. The pain of a broken love affair can make us feel as if life isn't worth living. But we must remember that the sun comes up in the morning, giving us the possibility of a beautiful day.

Rosa's suffering was very real. I could only hope she'd find peace within herself, not just from being accepted by her lovers. If she did, suicide wouldn't enter her mind. The choice was hers.

Tony Before and After

Tony took his life a few years ago. I think about him often with love and sadness. I've seen him twice since he committed suicide. His guilt and sorrow over this action breaks my heart.

Tony was a very talented and sensitive young man who seemed to have everything to live for. No one could blame this tragedy on the fact he'd received no help. He was in therapy four times a week and had many supportive friends who loved him. The fact was that when life became too difficult for Tony, he ended it. He wanted to die.

Suicide is rarely uncomplicated. The reasons for this action often stem back to childhood trauma, or even unresolved past-life experiences. I can't present a psychological study, since I'm not an expert in this field. I do wish to share my personal experiences with you in the hope you'll realize that suicide won't really solve any problems.

Tony wasn't a drinker or a drug abuser, was careful about his diet, and exercised regularly. He made a living as a professional actor, so he was very conscious of his looks.

Tony worried about *everything.* He could spend two hours in a store trying to decide between the blue and the black sweater. Then he'd spend another two hours wondering if he'd made the right choice. To say he was insecure is a gross understatement.

His insecurity stemmed from a need to have the approval of others, not from a personal sense of pride. One of the tragedies of his life was not knowing what a special person he was. No amount of support gave him confirmation. He couldn't be happy.

After fighting the demons within for thirty years, he took his life. People were shocked and angered. This was my first experience dealing with someone close who committed suicide. I was overwhelmed with grief. I wondered if I could have done more for him.

In time I received the answer.

Two years after his passing, Tony came to me through a message from a psychic in London. I was on vacation, visiting some friends. One of them told me about a wonderful psychic who lived right outside London. I made an appointment out of curiosity. It's always interesting to see how others in my profession work.

This British psychic told me there was someone very sad who wanted to give me a message from the spirit world.

"His name begins with a T. He's sorry that he caused

you pain. He knows now that what he did was wrong. He thanks you for all you did trying to help him."

Tears came to my eyes as I listened.

The psychic went on to say that Tony hadn't realized how many people loved him. Also that it had been awful for him to see the pain he caused his friends and family. He'd had no idea that anyone cared.

He says that it's cold and dim and lonely where he is. He wishes that he could go back and start over again. He feels stuck.

As I listened, I was overcome with sadness but comforted by my knowledge of reincarnation. Tony would be given the chance to live again. He wasn't in a hopeless situation, merely a tragic one.

The psychic continued. "He's crying and repeating over and over how sorry he feels. He's talked to some spirit helpers and this is getting him through until he can move into the spirit world. He knows how hard you tried to warn him about what would happen if he took his life, but at the time he was too self-involved to hear you."

The session ended. I walked through the streets of London reflecting on Tony's life and his present state of existence. Tony had always wanted others to make decisions for him. He refused to accept responsibility for his own life and his actions. He wasn't a bad person, just self-centered. Now he'd have to live between two worlds until it was time for his normal passing.

I would send loving thoughts in his direction, and hopefully they would give him a bit of comfort. In time he'd be all right.

The second message from Tony came about a year later as I walked past his apartment building in New

York. Being in his neighborhood always made me think about him. On this particular summer afternoon I walked by his building and was startled to see his spirit standing on the sidewalk. He didn't see me, which was just as well, since seeing me would have made him start apologizing again. I felt no angry feelings toward Tony, only regret. Although death had caused a great deal of suffering to the people who loved him, it also taught many lessons. One was that we could not blame ourselves for his decision. He'd been offered a great deal of help and chose not to accept it. One day he'd find the peace he'd been unable to achieve in his last earth life.

While We Live
We Have a Chance to Learn

Nora passed over from cancer six months ago. Though she suffered a great deal of pain during the last year of her life, she remained interested in everything and everyone. Her ability to be passionate about living despite the fact she was dying was an example to all who knew her. Her room was always overflowing with visitors.

Once a friend asked her how she kept from being depressed. "I don't enjoy the pain and sickness, but everything possible is being done for me. I think that every aspect of life is a wonder, and I don't want to waste a moment by being depressed."

When Nora passed over, she left the world a better place. She gave to others and learned from them until the moment of her passing. Sickness and pain didn't stop her from experiencing the wonder of life. Nora was a great lady who served through her life and through her death. Her cancer gave her the chance to rid herself of negative physical karma.

There are many theories as to what causes cancer. Diet and emotional outlook seem to be large factors in attracting this disease. But sometimes it's also a karmic situation. In Nora's case, I'm certain it was brought on from a past life. She lived a balanced, healthy life. But people must pass over from something, and this was Nora's way to go to the other side. I'm sure that next life she'll be blessed with good health. She has earned it!

What Constitutes Suicide?

What constitutes suicide? Is a death brought on by excessive behavior that could have been controlled a form of suicide? Are there suicides that don't seem obvious?

Harry

Harry was told over and over not to drink liquor because his liver was showing signs of damage. His doctor begged him to stop, warning him he'd die if he didn't. Harry's wife had tried everything in her power to get her husband to quit. No warning moved him. He continued to drink. Finally at the young age of forty-seven, he died.

Many of his friends called his death suicide. Was it? Harry didn't intend to kill himself. But he'd been given the opportunity through his doctor's warnings to change his habits and prolong his life. He'd be alive today if he'd stopped drinking.

I wasn't certain how I felt about situations like Harry's. Cases like Harry's aren't suicide in the conventional sense, yet self-destructive behavior can bring premature death. Many similar deaths could have been avoided by lifestyle changes.

I needed Lawrence's help to sort through this issue. I sent strong thoughts in his direction, knowing he'd respond when he could. He always appeared when he was needed.

Lake Placid

At the same time I felt the need to see Lawrence, I woke up with a desire to go to Lake Placid in upstate New York.

The urge was so strong that I rented a car and went. It's a lovely six-hour drive from the city. The leaves were golden and the air was crisp. I pulled up to the Mirror Lake Inn, a beautiful hotel I'd read about in a magazine. I'd been lucky; a room with an amazing view overlooking the lake was available. The Adirondack Mountains stood across from the lake.

I had needed a rest from the hectic pace of New York, and this was the perfect place. I unpacked and walked around town to look at the shops, had a quick lunch, and returned to my hotel.

The hotel had a beautiful library with stained-glass windows and a fireplace. I sat by the fire, staring into the flame, until a voice broke my concentration.

"I'm glad you could come to this lovely hotel. The service is wonderful and the clean air will do you a world of good."

It was Lawrence.

"I should have known, it was your thought patterns I was picking up, telling me to come here." I laughed.

We drank tea and enjoyed the beautiful fireplace. We discussed books and music. I filled him in on my work and life in general. It was rare that Lawrence talked about himself or his activities.

This day was an exception.

A LOOK INTO LAWRENCE'S LIFE

He'd been to Europe since we'd last seen each other. He was deeply interested in recent discoveries in the medical field. A close friend of his, a doctor in France, had been studying new pain medicines and their effect on the body. As Lawrence spoke, it was obvious that he had a strong medical background. I knew very little about his past and felt it wasn't my place to ask him personal questions. Today I eagerly listened.

I did know that he'd been raised in England in a happy home. His mother had a psychic gift, and his father was a doctor who inspired Lawrence, teaching a love of philosophy and imparting a thirst for knowledge. His love of knowledge had led Lawrence to the pursuit of the ancient wisdom. This was all he'd told me about himself prior to that day.

Today Lawrence told me that he, too, was a doctor. He'd studied medicine with his friend in France, but he'd never practiced. Once he completed the training he went on to learn other things. Feeling the need to do physical labor, he'd spent a year working on a farm in France. After France he went to India and spent ten years studying with various teachers. He said this was a remarkable period of his life.

He grew quiet and stared into the fire, then looked up at me and laughed. He knew that I had a million questions running through my mind.

"That's enough about my life for the moment. I'll tell you more at another time."

Lawrence said he had some letters to write and would meet me in the lobby at eight. I remained sitting in front of the fire, thinking about him.

He was elegant and mysterious but completely nonthreatening. It was obvious that he was highly educated, so it was not surprising that he'd been to medical school. To me he was a doctor of souls. His mere presence had a great healing quality. He could speak with authority on any subject. I tried to picture him working on a farm. I'm sure he was an example to all the other workers. He found the magic in everything, be it philosophy or a field of grain. He could love equally every action he performed. There was nothing in life that wasn't sacred to him. I was in awe of him but not intimidated by him. He possessed a greatness of soul that inspired me. It was a blessing to be in his company and an honor to be his student.

Everything that Lawrence did had a purpose. He chose to meet me in Lake Placid for a special reason and he talked about himself in order to teach me something. The reasons would be made clear in time. For the moment I was enjoying the peace and beauty of the library and the fire.

When I returned to my room to change for dinner, I found a beautiful bouquet of peach roses sitting on the desk next to my travel computer. The card next to them said: "All life can possess the beauty of a rose." There was no signature.

DINNER AT EIGHT

We met in the lobby and Lawrence said he knew of a little restaurant in Saranac Lake about eight miles away. We went out to get the car. It was a beautiful evening with a full moon; the air was crisp and clear.

The drive took about ten minutes. We stopped in front of a place called the Red Fox that reminded me of somewhere I'd been as a child in Iowa. A friendly woman led us to a corner table. The room was quite smoky, as there wasn't a no-smoking area. It was a steak house. I knew that Lawrence was a vegetarian, so it seemed an odd choice, but I trusted that he had his reasons for picking this particular restaurant.

The waitress told us her name was Arlene and asked if we would like cocktails. We ordered club sodas and said we'd wait a bit before ordering dinner. Lawrence then asked me how the book was progressing.

"Quite well, but I need to ask your opinion about something. A client of mine died from alcohol abuse. His doctor had warned him, even showed him X rays of his damaged liver, but Harry didn't even try to quit. Harry just kept on drinking, knowing full well that this could kill him. Is this a form of suicide?"

Lawrence thought for a moment, then spoke.

"One would have to examine the motive behind the deed. Did Harry drink with the intention of taking his life, or was it that he simply couldn't stop?"

"He didn't say he was going to drink himself into the grave, but he knew the doctor's warning was serious and that he'd live longer if he stopped. It's not unlike the diabetic who keeps eating sugar, knowing that it's killing him. It's the doctor's warning that bothered me. Many people don't get one. Harry respected and trusted the doctor. It's not easy to stop drinking or eating sugar, but Harry's life would've been prolonged if he'd changed his behavior."

"This isn't suicidal behavior, but it is self-destructive. There's a great difference between the two. Many people have self-destructive habits such as overeating, smoking, or excessive drinking, that can shorten their lives. These addictions stem from a lack of self-control, not a death wish. They must be conquered now or in a future life. Man often digs his grave with his desires and appetites." Lawrence stopped.

Isn't that the truth? I thought about people who passed over from lung cancer, heart attacks, liver failure, and other diseases that were the result of overindulgence in substances. My friend Liza cried about her mother's death from smoking. Everyone had tried to get this woman to stop but couldn't. Liza had called her mom's death suicide, but that wasn't necessarily the case: The woman didn't want to die, and it wasn't her intention to hurt anyone. She just didn't have the strength to quit.

There was also Gary, who died at age thirty of a heart attack after mixing drugs and alcohol at a party one night. He had had no previous heart trouble. Again, people called this suicide, but since he didn't do this with the intention of ending his life, it was actually a tragedy, not a suicide.

EUTHANASIA

I told Lawrence about some upsetting phone calls I'd been receiving. Some were from clients with terminal illnesses, such as cancer or AIDS; others were from family or friends of people who were gravely ill and in pain, who wanted my opinion on ending their lives. It was heartbreaking to me. Their greatest common fear was dying without dignity. The second concern was financial. Some had no money and no health insurance to pay for extended medical care.

I knew where I stood on this issue. I feel it is unacceptable to end your life, or to help someone else to end his because of illness. However, no one should be kept alive by the use of machines. Anyone who can't live without life-support systems should be allowed to pass over.

Matt, who was very sick with AIDS and getting worse every day, was angered by my opinion.

"It's hopeless, and now my mind is being affected. I'm in constant pain and life's no fun anymore. It's killing my mother to see me so sick. What's the point? I'm dying anyway." He was sobbing.

I'd received many calls from clients like Matt who had AIDS. It broke my heart to see young, talented, wonderful people afflicted with this horrible disease. I understood their terror and hopelessness, but suicide is not the answer. Dealing with AIDS, cancer, or any other serious illness is a challenge for all of us, a spiritual test. We must give all the love, support, and comfort we can to anyone with AIDS or any other terminal illness.

Our love can help them to overcome the desire to end their lives prematurely.

Susan couldn't bear watching her mother's pain from cancer. She didn't want her mom to die but didn't want her to continue suffering. Her mother's wish was to have Susan assist her with her death.

Susan did fulfill her mother's wish. After she'd given her mother the pills, she regretted it immediately. It took her mother many hours to pass over. Susan sat by her mother's bedside as she struggled for breath. When it was over, Susan didn't have a day's peace. Two years later she was diagnosed with cancer. She believed she'd attracted cancer because of grief and guilt over her mother's death.

Who can say for certain why Susan became ill? I can tell you that she never recovered from helping her mother die.

Lawrence was deeply moved by this conversation. He took my hand, and then with a great deal of passion said, "It's very difficult to deal with situations of this kind, but people must learn to think beyond the physical. It's often compassion that makes people believe that mercy killing is the right thing to do. But not always. Think of the abuses that could result if this were legalized. How many lives would be ended prematurely by so-called 'compassionate' friends and relatives? Who has the power to choose life or death for anyone? While we live, we're able to learn. There's karma involved with living and dying. If it's your karma to have a difficult death, it must be faced, or it will be repeated in a new life. I speak with true compassion, for I know that the suffering will be greater if life is ended before its natural time.

"There's no mercy in mercy killing. Suicide or assisted deaths aren't the end of suffering. They're the beginning of greater pain, a spiritual suffering. We must remember the pains of the physical are temporary; it's the spirit that suffers beyond the grave if you take your own life or assist someone in doing this."

THE RED FOXES

Our dinner arrived and we changed to a lighter subject. Lawrence told me more about his doctor friend in France, who was working around the clock developing less toxic pain medicines than those currently available. Lawrence had great respect for his French friend.

We finished our meal and ordered coffee.

I asked Arlene, the waitress, why the place was called the Red Fox.

She explained that there were red foxes out in the back.

I asked if they were dangerous.

"Not usually, but last year we did have some with rabies. One fox grabbed the purse right out of the hand of a woman as she was walking to her car. These foxes are known to be very shy. We knew something was wrong when their behavior changed and suddenly they became bold."

She walked away, shaking her head. Lawrence laughed but also pointed out the wisdom in that story.

"Think of how many problems could be avoided if we noticed when *people's* normal behavior changed."

He returned for a moment to the subject of suicide.

We talked about how often (but not always) one's behavior changes when an individual is suicidal. This is a red flag telling us our help is needed. Not all suicides can be prevented, but some could if we'd pay closer attention to the behavior of those around us. When people aren't operating with mental clarity, they need others to protect them. If someone stops sleeping, cries often and for no reason, or loses weight without dieting, direct them to a good doctor. A severely depressed person isn't always able to call for aid. It could be our good fortune to help someone avoid suicide, thus saving them from suffering a void in the spirit world.

We asked for the check and left the restaurant. We drove slowly back to the hotel, enjoying the ride.

I was thinking about our discussion of suicide, and another question came to my mind.

"Lawrence, does it make a difference if someone is insane when they end their life? I know that some people are quite sane when they suicide and some aren't."

"The state that one lives in, temporarily, as a result of suicide, varies according to the suicide's character. Each person will remain in an uncomfortable state between earth and spirit until the time of their natural passing. Insanity doesn't change this, but not all states are exactly the same. Some people will be overwhelmed with guilt and remorse, and some will appear a bit dazed, as if in a fog. Each person will be given many chances to live again. They'll be able to find forgiveness from those they have harmed, and from themselves."

We arrived back at the hotel. Lawrence said he wouldn't see me in the morning, since he had to leave.

He advised me to rest for two more days and promised to be in touch again very soon.

I walked into my room and was cheered by the roses. Lawrence had known that I'd be sad when he left, so he gave me the roses. I'm sure he'd taken me to the Red Fox just so I could hear the waitress's story about the red foxes. He had a reason for everything, and although I didn't always know what it was at the moment, in time everything was made clear.

Joy

I was able to use Lawrence's wisdom immediately upon my return to New York. Mark, a client I'd known for years, was frantic. His wife Joy's behavior had changed noticeably within the last few weeks. Mark didn't know how to cope with her. He was timid by nature and hated confrontation. Joy, on the other hand, could be quite intimidating when she wanted to be. Normally she was very tidy in her grooming and housekeeping. Now she was walking around in dirty clothes with unkempt hair, leaving dishes in the sink and things all over the floor. If Mark tried to pick anything up, Joy yelled at him. He'd asked Joy's mother to help, but she didn't want to get involved. Finally Mark begged me to help him. Since Joy wouldn't come to my place, I went over to see them at their apartment.

The place was a wreck and Joy seemed even worse than Mark had described. I tried to chat with her, but she seemed to be in another world. Mark was a bundle of nerves on the verge of tears. I knew Joy needed to see a doctor, but it wouldn't be easy to get her to agree.

As I sat in the living room with Joy I saw a woman

very clearly, in spirit, next to Joy. The woman was shaking her head, and appeared very worried. I watched her closely, hoping for some message to help us. Then I heard a voice in my head say, "Call her Heidi, that's what I used to call her. It was her favorite children's story. I read it every night. Tell Heidi that Gram wants her to see a doctor. She always did what I told her to do when she was little. Go on." The voice stopped and the image faded away.

I looked at Joy and said, "Heidi, your gram wants you to go to the doctor."

"Where is she?" Joy jumped up and started looking around.

"I think she may be at the doctor's, Joy. Let's go and see."

Mark looked shocked but said nothing. He waited. Joy seemed a bit confused but agreed to go with us. We took her to a psychiatrist, who discovered she was reacting to a medication that had been prescribed for a minor medical problem. He said she could've become suicidal if we'd waited any longer.

We'd have to thank her grandma, since she was the one who got Joy to the doctor.

Once off the medication, Joy returned to her old self. Joy was one of the lucky ones: Her loved ones here and in spirit were looking out for her.

The Bigger Picture

It's possible to face physical and emotional trials with understanding instead of hopelessness if we can see and accept the bigger picture. The problems that drive people to take their lives are temporary. Life itself is eternal.

We must face the tests brought to us by our own karma. These tests give us the opportunity to produce new karma, and to release past karma.

This one short earth life is a drop of water in the ocean of time. We are born, live, and pass on into the spirit world. Death is as natural as birth, and we should die as naturally as possible. In a natural death the spirit floats calmly toward the light. In a suicide the soul is ripped from the body.

We're never too young to learn. Children and teenagers can be taught the sacredness of life. They can be given coping tools to help them through life's trials. Educating people about the bigger picture can help avoid many suicides.

Suicide doesn't end our problems, it only intensifies them. I can't emphasize enough that you can't kill anything. You can stop your physical life but you are still alive in spirit.

Talk to people who've tried to take their lives and failed. They'll confirm that the place they went to wasn't a happy one and that they're grateful to have been given another chance at life.

Troubles pass but the God within remains. We must protect life to show respect to the God that lives within us.

Even if you discover you've got only a few months to live, you should use the time to gather as much knowledge as you can to help you in your next life.

The physical body begins to die the moment we're born. Everything that we do in life we do while we're in the process of physical dying. Until we draw our last breath we can learn and experience from life. We can love and serve others and the God within. All of life is sacred and full of wonder, and must be preserved.

The bigger picture is painted by all our actions. We earn our next life by the way we live and die in this one.

* 6

The World of Thought

The spirit world is a world of thought. The moment you arrive into spirit, your complete realization of the power of thought will overwhelm you. You may have read every book on the market about the power of positive thinking, but on the other side it's even greater than you can imagine.

After you arrive in spirit, you'll immediately see the action of your thought. You are no longer restricted by your physical body. On earth we must first think about doing something, then perform the physical action in order to put the thought to work. Let's say you decide to go to the store. You must leave your house and drive or walk to the site. In spirit you would think about being somewhere and actually be there at the same moment. Mind and thought are one; they're a team.

Positive thinking in physical life helps to create a happy, fulfilling life. Thinking positive thoughts can help get us through our troubles and affect the quality of our life and our afterlife. The circumstances of our physical life are a combination of our current thinking and actions and past-life karmic situations brought into this life. Certain situations we must deal with in our earth life aren't just the result of our thinking habits;

they're karmic. When we arrive into spirit, our life consists exclusively of our thoughts. Karma is worked through only in the physical.

Right Thinking

A lovely woman named Carrie passed over from cancer in 1989. I'd spent a great deal of time with her during her illness, and we'd discussed the other side many times. She knew that positive thinking would help her through her trials, and was very diligent in her application of positive thoughts. She wouldn't allow herself to think thoughts that were angry and resentful. She kept her mind focused on ways to promote health. Carrie was a person who always saw the glass as half full, not half empty. Everyone loved Carrie and many tried to emulate her positive persona. Her nickname, Angel, suited her well.

Carrie had been in remission for two years and was devastated when the cancer recurred. She felt responsible. She thought that she hadn't been positive enough, and because of this the cancer returned. She broke down and cried. "Why won't my body behave like my mind tells it to?" Her feelings of guilt saddened me. She'd gotten the wrong idea about positive thinking, and I wanted to help her understand it. There'd been no problem with her thinking. She was one of the most positive, loving people I'd ever met. She never complained about her illness, and helped others in any way she possibly could. Her cancer was karmic.

I explained to her that there are certain situations in our lives that we carry over from a past life. For example, a baby is born blind. The mother took good care of her health during the pregnancy. No other family member is blind. There is no logical reason for this seeming injustice. The fact is, the soul of this child brought this problem with him in order to release the karma from a past life. Who can accuse a baby of wrong thinking?

As the baby grows, the choice of how to deal with his karmic situation is in his hands. Positive thinking will help him to face this challenge with humor and courage. Will he become angry if positive thinking doesn't restore his sight? Or will he be a happy, productive person living with his karmic problem? The answer lies in his thinking habits.

Carrie was greatly relieved as she accepted the fact that she'd done everything possible in her power to restore health. We examined her life and her way of thinking, and she saw clearly that she'd lived a very good, positive life. This put her at peace with her death.

I received a message from Carrie after her passing. This came to me in an interesting manner. Before Carrie passed over we'd discussed the fact that we'd see each other again. She told me that when she passed, she'd let me know. There would be a clear sign showing me that all was well.

Carrie lived in California, so I wasn't with her the day she passed over. Late the night of her passing, as I was in my bedroom watching TV a Baccarat crystal angel (that usually sits on my dresser) flew across the room. It literally flew. (I'm used to this type of phenomena. They aren't uncommon to psychics.) I picked up the angel, and as I replaced it I saw White Feather standing next to my desk. His arms were folded. His calm demeanor alerted me that there was a message.

I became quite still and focused all my concentration onto my astral screen. I saw Carrie's face illuminated. She was laughing and talking with a group of people. Her mother was one of the group. (I'd seen the mother's picture. She'd passed over when Carrie was ten years old.) It looked like a big party. Carrie, who'd been very thin and gray, now looked perfectly healthy. Positive thinking and her belief in the afterlife helped to make her transition into spirit clear and smooth. This picture showed that she was ready to pass over. Her thoughts at the time of her death were as positive as they'd been during her life.

The picture faded and White Feather had gone. I looked at the clock, thinking I should call her husband. It was midnight in California, so I decided to wait until the following day to call.

The next morning my phone rang. Carrie's husband called to tell me that his "angel" had passed over at approximately midnight. He confirmed that she was in a calm, peaceful state as she let go of the physical.

I didn't tell him that I already knew.

Manifestation of Thought in Spirit

On earth, thoughts must take a concrete, physical form in order to be effective. This isn't the case in spirit.

In the physical world, for example, you must work hard to create a home. The plans are drawn, then executed by a builder. It can take months of hard labor to bring a home to life, not to mention furnishing it.

In spirit you simply think of the house you'd like and it's yours. Grandma Grace reproduced her Iowa home in spirit by thinking about it. Her desire to live in this familiar setting manifested it. The house is very real, but it's not composed of physical matter: It's composed of thought forms. The house will remain as long as Grandma's thought forms desire it to be there. In time she may outgrow her desire for this house, and it will vanish. Gram's thought forms will tell people where she is. A thought directed to her, with force, will be received by her. If a person Gram knew on earth arrives into spirit and wants to know where she's living, this person sends her a powerful thought. Gram receives it, then, using her own powerful thought forms, Grandma sends directions to the house. This all happens instantaneously. Gram's friend then decides how to get to the house. She can walk if she wishes, or she can fly.

Just because your thoughts are manifested doesn't mean that one has no privacy in spirit. The spirit dweller doesn't suddenly become clairvoyant and able to read everyone else's thoughts. It would be hard to feel blissful if you felt your thoughts weren't your own. What happens is that you see the results of your thoughts without performing a physical action. Thought forms manifest instantaneously. If you think about a type of clothing you'd like to wear, you're wearing it. If you concentrate on a person you'd like to communicate with, instantly you'll receive a message from them.

FLYING

We can move instantaneously in spirit with no delay in time. You simply focus your mind upon the place you'd like to be and you are instantly there. Our minds control our bodies. While in the physical we must wait for our bodies to move; wishing won't get us where we want to go. The spirit body and the mind are partners. They work together simultaneously.

Some people who arrive into spirit must learn this new way of moving. You often feel clumsy until you are comfortable with the mind-body connection. Remember the case of Molly. (She had the near-death experience and brought me the message from "the old lady.") Her uncle had to hold her so she wouldn't fall while they were moving. This being her first trip into the spirit world, she didn't yet understand the power of the mind. She didn't have the time to become used to the instantaneous action. But nobody is injured from falling in spirit, as the spirit body can't be harmed.

Many reports from those who've had a near-death experience talk of the fast movement, or say they felt as if they were flying. The quickness of movement in the visions that White Feather showed me impressed me. In a flash the scene would change. I learned that happened because thought and action aren't separated in spirit as they are in the physical world.

Maria

A young woman of twenty-three reported this near-death experience to me.

"I recall being in my living room, feeling very faint.

I called to my husband for help. The next thing I knew I was above my body, looking down at it. For a second I felt out of balance, as if I could fall, but that feeling passed quickly. I thought about my baby upstairs and found myself immediately in the baby's room. The baby was fine, sleeping soundly. My mind went back to my husband, and in a flash I was standing back in the living room, watching him, giving me mouth-to-mouth resuscitation. The phone rang, and I was instantly in the kitchen next to the telephone. It was amazing. I felt free as a bird, and kept flying around my house, watching everything. My next recollection was waking up in the hospital."

She told her husband everything that she'd seen during the time she was supposedly dead. He was shocked by her detailed description, but he accepted this as proof of life after death.

Six months after Maria's near-death experience her husband died in a car accident. Maria was grief-stricken and very lonely. They'd been together for nine years and she loved him very much. But she was greatly comforted by her near-death experience, and felt that God had blessed her. She knew that her husband wasn't dead, but free from earthly worries. And she's sure that he's able to fly.

THOUGHT FORMS

Every thought you have—in spirit and in the physical— takes a form. These forms can be seen by the trained psychic. The intensity of the thought determines the weight, power, and shape of this form.

Some thoughts that pass through our minds quickly

don't create lasting forms. Others, because of their intensity or because of repetition, will become a powerful form with color and sound. This form remains with us and affects our lives. For example, if you drop a burning cigarette ash on your coat and immediately brush it off, odds are it won't burn a hole in your clothing. If you let it sit, it'll burn right through, leaving a hole in your garment. It is the same with a thought. The longer you hold the thought, the more power it builds. Thoughts, like fire, have little effect if they're not allowed to linger. Thoughts that are held create strong patterns that build our auras. (The aura is a colored cloudlike substance—created by our thoughts, feelings, and passions—that surrounds our bodies. This sensitive atmosphere responds immediately to emotional and thought changes, and with emotional change the color changes.)

Different thoughts resonate differently: Intense jealousy creates a brownish-green, murky color in the aura of the person holding this type of thought. As you hold this thought, all good thoughts directed toward you will be repelled by this negative one. A loving thought will produce shades of yellow and will open you to attract other positive thoughts.

Let's say you feel an intense hatred toward someone. You think over and over about your disdain for this person. This negativity will assume a nasty form and an angry red color in your aura. If you hold on to the anger for a long time, no loving person will be attracted to you.

You don't have to be a psychic to know that spending time with a depressed, negative person will bring you down too. This happens because you are in their aura and, like a chameleon, you can't help absorbing their vibration.

The power of your will is the only tool for breaking a negative pattern. You must replace the hateful thought with one of love or forgiveness. If you're unable to do so, it's possible you'll become mentally unbalanced. In any case, you'll definitely be unhappy, as wrong thinking creates nothing but suffering.

Good thoughts will create positive forms and the result will be happiness and balance. This is true in both the physical and spirit worlds.

You must have clairvoyant gifts in order to see thought forms. They aren't discernible to the physical eye until they're given concrete expression. If you don't possess these gifts, you must wait to hear or to see the physical result of thought forms. The power of thinking is a great deal more obvious in the spirit world.

HOW PSYCHICS READ THOUGHT FORMS

Understanding thought forms may help you better to understand one way that a psychic gift works: It's really a matter of vibration.

Everything is alive and vibrates at different rates. The clairvoyant has the ability to perceive things at a different rate of vibration. For example, a woman who I've never seen before comes in for a session. She's dressed nicely and appears to be fine.

But I look at her and see an angry vibration: Its color is red and it vibrates rage. Next, I am able to pick up the circumstances of the anger. She's just broken up with her boyfriend, who's been cheating on her. She wants revenge.

This comes to me as easily as reading a book because I'm tuning into her thought forms. I can then psychically perceive her future as it is headed. I see that she will become ill if she holds on to this negative thinking. But she has free will to change this course by altering her thinking. In this case she can force herself to replace her feelings of anger with ones of forgiveness.

As we talk, other thought forms come into being, but anger remains dominant. The other forms can't compete with the power of her rage. Hopefully, time will heal her thinking. What's the point of holding on to this negativity? She'll be the one to suffer for it.

I try to help her understand the need to change her thinking. But she doesn't see what I mean. She knows that she's very unhappy and obsessed with her rage. But this doesn't prove to her that negative thinking is directly responsible for her unhappiness. Time will provide the proof she's seeking.

You create your world by the way you think. You have free will to choose the way you think about any situation in your life. We can't always change our circumstances, but we can change our thinking. Lawrence has often said, "It doesn't matter what happens as much as how we react to what happens." In spirit this is well known, but we on earth are just beginning to learn.

S.O.S.

I've spoken about my thought connection with Lawrence. He's able to pick up my thought forms instantly when I direct them toward him with power. This takes concentration and purpose on my part. I think about him, letting him know I would welcome his help, and he receives this immediately. He decides if it's necessary for us to meet.

Sometimes he returns my cry for help with a loving thought form. When he does this, I feel wrapped in a blanket of comfort. Other times he just shows up. Sometimes it seems that he doesn't respond. The truth is, he answers by saying nothing. His silence lets me know that I can handle the particular situation myself. A wise teacher allows the student to find his own solutions to problems whenever possible.

It would be selfish of me to call upon Lawrence for every little problem that arises. I do my best to call upon him only if things seem especially troublesome.

Lawrence has total control over his thinking. His motivation in all things is selfless. His thinking is on an elevated level.

"Most people can't control their thoughts, so they're controlled by them," he's told me many times.

He's warned me to be aware of my thinking at all times.

"We must aspire to keep our thinking on a spiritual level. Obsessive thinking creates imbalance and disharmony. Work to train your thinking the way a dancer trains his body to respond to his command. This takes concentration and discipline. Command your mind to think of love, not hate, to think of forgiveness, not of anger or revenge. This will serve to make this life and future ones better."

The spirit world has no industry and no money changing hands, so there are no thoughts of greed or competition. The spirit body doesn't require food, so thoughts about eating aren't created. The spirit body remains in perfect health, so there's no need to think about diet or exercise. The materialist may think this sounds rather dull, as he can't conceive of life without the pursuit of physical pleasures. Yet the spirit world is alive with thoughts of love directed toward the quest for knowledge. We are served by keeping our thoughts ones of beauty. We can be harmed by holding thoughts aimed at fulfilling physical pleasure.

Visiting the Spirit Realms During Sleep

I've mentioned that some of my psychic experiences and visions come to me through dreams. The spirit body often travels during sleep. The cord that connects the physical and spirit bodies is quite elastic. During sleep I've traveled to the spirit realms guided by White Feather or a friend who has passed on. It's possible to move between worlds quite smoothly during sleep, as we're not overloaded with thoughts of physical activities.

I spent many years studying my dreams. I trained myself to wake up and record my dreams immediately after they ended. My dream life is very active. Some nights I wake up five or six times.

Life is very hectic for most of us and mine is no exception. I think that sometimes the only way that the departed can get through to me is when I'm sleeping.

Being a psychic can be like having a phone line that's constantly busy. In an emergency it's necessary to have the operator break into a call. Sometimes a soul on the other side must break into my sleep in order to relay a message. There aren't enough hours in the day to attend to everything, so the nights are used.

Each night before I go to sleep, I send positive thoughts to White Feather and to Lawrence. This little ritual helps to release any thought forms that can interfere with my ability to receive messages from those who may need me. This very simple act is very effective.

Our thoughts are alive during sleep.

David

My friend David, who passed over several months ago, came to me a few weeks ago in a dream. He was very funny on earth and he's retained his sense of humor in spirit.

He started by scolding me, telling me that I'm impossible to reach.

"There's a line of people waiting to make contact with you. I thought I'd never get through to you. Did you like the way I made the picture break the day I passed over?" (He had knocked over a picture in my living room.)

"I didn't enjoy spending the money to have the glass replaced. Wasn't there another sign you could have used?" I joked with him.

He reminded me that it was my own fault. I had told him that pictures fall and glass breaks when we pass over because people relate to those signs. They have been used over and over throughout history as signs to herald death, so why bother changing something that's recognizable?

David then became serious and talked about his happiness in the spirit world. He'd asked permission from my teacher, "the old lady," to speak to me, and she'd helped him to make the contact with me.

David had been very afraid of passing over, even after I explained to him about the spirit world and that we don't really die. I promised him that his fear would leave him at the moment of his passing.

He made this visit to thank me for helping him, as he didn't get the opportunity to do this before he passed over.

I woke from this dream and the same picture that broke when David passed over had moved from the wall and was lying next to my bed. This time the glass wasn't broken.

My Visit with "the Old Lady"

I've told you about the messages Molly and David got from "the old lady" for me. Now I'd like to tell you about my personal visit with her.

Molly saw "the old lady" sitting in the boardroom. This is the place in spirit where teachers gather together in order to make decisions to help us on earth. It's a very large room with an extremely long table surrounded by many chairs. There are many different teachers with expertise on specific subjects. They gather together to discuss ideas for inspiring mankind.

White Feather showed me this room when I was very young. At the time I didn't quite understand its importance. Now it's very clear to me. The teachers decide what philosophies might be tried to help humanity. The joint decision to inspire someone on earth to start a new religion or a new type of psychology is made in this room.

The person on earth receives the inspiration from the teachers because it's his or her karma to do so. The teachers can't interfere with the karma of the planet. Nothing is started that we on earth haven't earned the right to have.

People ask how the teachers can allow suffering on earth. The answer lies in understanding that man learns from all the experiences that he attracts to himself. No teacher wants anyone to suffer, but no one can interfere with the karma we have created for ourselves by our own actions.

In 1990 I was very sick with pneumonia. I've been blessed with good health, so this illness was very unusual. I felt very tired and had a high fever. The doctor had given me medication, so there wasn't anything to do except rest.

It's a fact that sometimes when we're ill our psychic perceptions are sharper. This may seem odd, yet it's true. I believe that when illness occurs, our defenses are down, so there's less of a barrier between worlds.

I was in bed, dozing, and suddenly I felt as if I were floating. Pictures flew in front of me quickly. I wasn't dying or having a near-death experience. I was a psychic viewing the astral plane in living color from my Greenwich Village apartment. I tuned in to the astral plane and could see everything as if it were a movie on TV. I stopped at the boardroom and saw "the old lady" writing with a quill pen. She was so involved in her work that she didn't seem to notice me. The papers were flying all over the room and she didn't appear to be concerned. I wanted to speak to her, but I felt shy.

She then stopped writing and looked directly at me.

"Well, I see you've finished your first book. It's about time!" she exclaimed, then she smiled. Her glow seemed to fill the universe.

I'd expected this dear woman to be harsh, as I'd read many reports of her temper.

She then explained the boardroom and what the teachers do there. She told me things that I was to do when I felt better. She showed me the paper she was working on.

"It'll be published down there when the time is right." ("Down there" is how she referred to the earth plane.)

I'll never forget the love that shone in her eyes when she looked at me. This look has served to give me strength in times of need.

I was then aware of my bedroom, and that the phone was ringing. On the bed next to me was a feather that looked as if it came from a quill pen! She'd sent me back to earth with a gift from the other side.

Freedom

I was quite young when I first experienced the power of thought. This has stayed with me my whole life.

For a period of time everything I desired showed up. The silliest things, such as an address book or a wallet, would appear if I thought about them. I recall thinking one day, "I must go and buy a new address book." Then I walked outside, and sitting next to the front door was a new address book still covered in plastic. At first it just seemed like an odd coincidence, so I'd shrug it off.

But after this kind of thing happened ten times I really observed my thinking. I saw that if I held a thought for any length of time, things would manifest. This wasn't good, as I knew that thought forms were being created in order to bring these things to me.

I didn't intend to misuse the force, it was just happening. The fact that I have psychic gifts make my thought patterns more intense than those of most people, so I must observe my thinking more closely than others.

I learned through discipline to control my thinking. I don't hold any thought in order to get anything. I do the best I can to keep my thinking positive, productive, and kind. This will allow anything that's mine to come naturally.

Thoughts are very potent. They are the road to freedom.

We're not free if we are obsessed by anything, be it a substance or a person or a desire for material gain. All these imbalances are created by our thinking. Imagine that! We can change our lives by changing the way we think. This doesn't imply that thinking alone will bring forth all the things we desire. If you are thinking properly, you're not overloaded with the desire for anything. We learn to desire nothing except peace of mind. In this way freedom will be ours.

Physical existence makes this type of thinking difficult. We are constantly being tested by the temptations of the physical world. Desire is a major cause of premature death, sickness, and decay. Isn't it a freeing thought to realize that in spirit we're no longer burdened by these temporary things?

In spirit we're no longer exhausted by the pursuit of

temporary pleasures. The spirit body doesn't have to fight for anything. Freedom from the addictions and stresses of physical life is ours once we enter the heavenly realms. We would be well served if we started our positive thinking patterns right now. There's nothing gained by delaying.

Think Before You Act

In the physical world we're served by thinking before we act. In spirit, thoughts and action occur at the same moment. Our motivation in spirit isn't for physical gain. We don't have to live with the constant fear that we did or said something wrong. These mistakes belong to the physical world. This is a major part of heavenly bliss.

Gloria

Gloria passed over into spirit recently. I was sitting at the computer, working, when the phone rang. Although I screen my calls when I'm writing and rarely listen to messages until the end of the day, something made me listen to this message. It was Gloria's son letting me know that the end for his mother was near. She wanted to say good-bye. She was too weak to hold the phone, so her son held the receiver to her ear and we spoke.

I'd met her in Santa Fe in 1987 and she'd been a warm, generous friend. She hadn't felt well for a long time and had tried everything to get better. It was now obvious that nothing would prolong her life, so she was letting those close to her say good-bye. Her son, a doctor, did everything known to medicine to help his mom and he was at peace that it was in God's hands.

"Please don't be afraid, Gloria. You're not alone" were the first words out of my mouth.

"I'm not afraid, but I don't think I'm ready to go today," she whispered.

She then added, "I wanted to read your book on the afterlife before I went."

"You know everything that you need to, Gloria. We've talked about all this many times. I'm going to ask White Feather, my guide, to be with you." I held back tears, wishing I could be with her.

"Would he do that for me?" She seemed in awe.

"Of course, Gloria," I added.

"Mary, what should I think about as I wait to pass over?"

"Gloria, you're one of the finest people I've ever met. You've had a wonderful life. You must just think about the beauty that awaits you in the spirit world. Think about those who are in spirit that you've missed. They'll be waiting at the border to greet you."

Her son came back on the line, as his mother wasn't able to talk any longer. He thanked me, and said his mother seemed at peace.

I sat quietly and sent thought forms to my guide, White Feather. I asked him to please go to Gloria, as it would give her great comfort. As I sat in quiet contemplation I heard him say, "I am with her now."

A strong feeling of calm came over me. Gloria would feel White Feather's presence, and this would aid her on her journey. We'd known each other for a long time and Gloria knew about my guide and was very respectful toward him. She would begin to see the other side as she began the transition from earth to spirit. She'd enter the world of thought smoothly and happily.

Two days after Gloria's passing, a dear friend of mine, Smitty, an astrologer who lives in the Napa Valley, called. (I'd introduced Gloria and her daughter to Smitty and they'd both had readings with her.) Before I could tell Smitty about Gloria's passing, she spoke. "Mary T., there was a very large, serious Indian dressed totally in white here yesterday. I felt that he was a guide of yours. I was with a client of mine who's very ill and the Indian's presence had a very strong healing effect."

Smitty wasn't surprised when I explained that White Feather had gone to California to see Gloria. It seems that he visited two of my dear friends while he was there.

Visions

The difference between dreams and visions is that we must sleep in order to dream, while visions come to us both in sleep and while awake. Visions come to me in different ways. The astral screen is the vehicle of projection. They come in flashes or sometimes they remain for longer moments. They aren't always pictures of the other side. Sometimes they depict scenes of this side. These are ways in which the psychic nature imparts knowledge.

These visions are comprised of thought forms sent to me through pictures. Thought forms can be sent through words, pictures, or sounds. The receiver has the gift of tuning in to vibrations, much like a radio.

Some visions are seen in the mind's eye. The mind's eye creates pictures in the brain. These are a different type of vision, as they aren't projected on a screen, giving them a life outside of the mind. All these images are a product of thought forms. These thought forms can be sent from someone, or I can tune in to them through concentration.

Who Gives and Receives Messages

Those who live in spirit aren't always close enough to pick up our thought forms. My teachers and those who've contacted me have a purpose when they do so: They desire to educate others by giving messages to me.

Two kinds of spirit folks can give and receive messages. The first are those of a high spiritual development. "The old lady" and White Feather are examples of this type of spirit messenger.

Souls who remain in realms close to the earth are the other type. There are different reasons for remaining in these spheres: The soul may be connected to friends or family by thought forms sent because of grief, anger, or loss. These forms keep the spirit from resting in peace, as the spirit is disrupted by the heartbreak of those who can't let them go.

Luke

A client, Luke, came for a session in a severe depression. He'd lost his wife and couldn't get over the loss. Grief is normal and necessary, but Luke was in danger of becoming ill or unbalanced by his overwhelming despair. He'd seen a therapist and was attending a support group for those who've lost loved ones. He'd found no comfort with these support systems. A friend suggested that a session with me might be helpful.

Luke walked into my apartment, sat down, and began to cry.

"I just don't know how to go on without her," he said between sobs.

I waited for a few minutes and spoke.

"Luke, I know that you feel very empty and alone, but you must understand that your wife can't find peace if you are so very unhappy. She'll be able to feel your unhappy thought forms and there's little she can do for you. Don't you want to help her? I know that it's not easy, but it's a great act of love to let those we love go. Please don't misunderstand and think I don't feel your pain. I just want you to help your wife to rest in peace."

Luke had heard me, and stopped crying for a moment.

"Is that true that my wife can be upset because of my sadness? I thought that when they were gone that was it."

"Luke, thought forms as powerful as yours can be received by your wife in spirit. This isn't to imply that she's earthbound. The veil between the worlds is very thin. Thought of a powerful nature can cut through this veil and be picked up by a soul in the spirit world."

Luke sat in silence for a moment and then said, "I don't believe you."

His disbelief was normal. People find it difficult to believe what can't be seen by their eyes. Grief made his blindness deeper. His anger and loss clouded his faith.

I was looking at Luke, feeling a great deal of sympathy, when I felt a presence in the room. A cool breeze alerted me that there was a visitor from the other side.

In my mind's eye I saw a woman who looked about forty, with a thick mane of red hair, and she was holding a candle. A voice in my head clearly said, "Luke, don't be sad. I'm keeping the candle lit until you join me. I'm fine and it's more beautiful here than you can imagine. Don't think such upsetting thoughts, they'll keep you from feeling happiness. It's very difficult for me to feel joy knowing that you're in such misery." The image faded.

I relayed this message to Luke, who was visibly shaken. He told me that he and his wife always kept a candle lit until they were both home. It had started as a romantic ritual and became a habit. Luke stressed the fact that no one knew about this.

"Luke, it wouldn't have given you faith and confirmation that your wife is alive in spirit unless she'd sent a message that was yours alone." I paused.

He then became paranoid. "How did you do that?"

"It's part of the psychic gift. You earned the right to receive a message from your wife. It was your thought forms that brought her here today. I was the conduit that received her thought forms from the spirit world. It's quite simple, yet hard for people to accept. This wasn't my doing. Your wife decided to send the message. I'd never try to draw anyone back to the earth sphere. I think it's unkind. You should be grateful. Few people are as fortunate as you and receive messages from the other side." I stopped.

Luke left the session angry. He kept asking over and over how I'd known about the candle. I'd never seen this man before and couldn't remember the friend who referred him to me. I've been seeing clients for over twelve years, and it's impossible to remember everyone. Luke still wanted physical explanations for things of a spiritual nature. He wasn't able to accept this lovely message with gratitude. I felt sorry for him. With such poor thinking habits, his life would remain difficult. I'd done what I knew was necessary. At least his wife could now rest in peace. She'd keep the candle glowing in her heart until they were reunited. Then Luke would have his answers.

How to Change Your Life

We can rebuild our worlds by changing our thoughts. In the spirit world nothing matters except the power of love.

Heaven is the plane of consciousness of love built by thought. Our world is formed by our thinking. Positive thinking always has a healing quality. You're building thought forms that will live with you after your body is discarded.

Although karma dictates many of the circumstances of our lives, there are also many situations that can be changed by altering our thinking.

Vicki

A client named Vicki came to see me for the third time. Her last appointment had been a year and a half earlier. She hardly looked like herself! I didn't recognize her.

She was twenty pounds thinner, with a new hairdo and a new disposition.

I commented that she seemed like a different person.

"Do you remember the last time I was here?" she asked.

"I remember that you were very depressed and had negative and hopeless feelings and that you became angry with me."

"You told me to stop feeling sorry for myself because I didn't have any problems that couldn't be solved." She laughed.

"Looks like you took the advice."

Vicki left my place that first day feeling angry and frustrated, thinking that I was insensitive to her needs. I had told her that she must change her thinking in order to change her world. She should wake up each day and spend a few minutes thinking of all the things she had to be grateful for. This seemed incredibly corny to her, but something compelled her to try.

She worked hard to change her thoughts from ones of self-pity to ones of action. Slowly, her life started to turn around. Things that had seemed very difficult were starting to be easier. For example, dieting had always been very hard and suddenly it wasn't. She started thinking about being good to her body instead of constantly abusing it with too much food, and the weight began to drop off. She developed a little positive saying for herself: "All that is mine will come to me. I must be the best person that I can be today." And if things became difficult, she would repeat it.

It wasn't just Vicki's weight loss that was obvious, it was the spiritual weight loss that made the difference.

She'd been carrying the weight of her negative thinking and now this burden was shed.

Everything in her life was better. She was ecstatic.

She hadn't spent time asking for specific things to come to her. She concentrated on being the best Vicki possible.

Each of us can have a powerful effect on our lives and those around us by developing good thought habits. These habits will die with us and help us to pass over with ease.

> "As man thinketh in his heart, so is he."
> —Proverbs 23; verse 7

He was teaching us that our lives are deeply affected by our thoughts. We are a synthesis of our thoughts from this life and our past ones. We incarnate with the patterns of our thoughts from past lives, and these form the basis for the events of this life. We don't bring in our bodies from other lives, nor our bank accounts. We bring only our karma created by the actions performed, motivated by our thinking habits. Our character is the sum total of our thoughts.

We arrive into spirit with the character we took from the earth.

I once asked Lawrence, "How can we best prepare for the transition to the other side?"

This is what he told me:

"You prepare for dying by living a life with proper thinking.

"You can prepare for death as you should prepare for sleep. There's little difference between the two. When you sleep you wake up on this side, when you die you wake up on the other side.

"In order to have a good night's sleep you should release any anger or negativity. Never go to sleep until you've forgiven any wrongs done to you. Never go to sleep without gratitude for all the joys of life. Before sleeping, observe your thoughts and focus them on things of beauty. This action will insure that you wake up refreshed. Your thoughts have a powerful life in the sleep state, and this power is intensified during your waking hours.

"If you can sleep in peace, you can die with peace.

"It's all in the way that you think about it."

✳ 7

Prescription for Grief

When my friend Nicky passed over, I cried a great deal. I was very happy that he was no longer afraid or in pain, but I missed him. For at least six months after his passing I'd find myself picking up the phone to call him and then remembering that he was no longer here. All of us who loved him helped each other deal with the loss. We talked about him and what he'd meant to us. We didn't suppress our emotions; we cried together and at times we laughed. Nicky left us with wonderful memories, many touching and an equal number humorous. Time helped heal the pain of his loss.

Grieving is an unavoidable part of life. Grief is painful and not always rational in its expressions. Sometimes we feel that our mourning period has ended, then the grief returns without warning. Grief can show its face in a movie theater or on hearing a familiar song. Months after Nicky's passing, his favorite song came over the radio and the grief of loss returned to me.

Nicky had gone on to a better life, but he'd left an empty space in mine. His sister sent me one of his favorite objects, a gold feather. Nicky had known about White Feather and bought his feather as a respectful acknowledgment of his spirituality. I held this object that radiated Nicky's vibration and cried again.

Grief is a great but difficult teacher. It is a battle we must fight. It can be won through talking, crying, time, and helping each other. The grieving process demands that we reflect upon the temporary state of physical life. We are focused to understand that we can't possess anyone and we are asked to say good-bye.

My tears weren't for Nicky, they were for my personal loss and for all those who missed him.

We must give ourselves permission to grieve. If we don't express our sadness, hurt, and anger, we can become depressed. If we suppress our feelings, they won't go away: They will rear their angry heads no matter how hard we try to avoid them.

> O time! thou must untangle this, not I;
> It is too hard a knot for me to untie.
> —Shakespeare, *Twelfth Night*

People require different amounts of time for grieving. We must be patient with those who are in pain. It's tempting to want to say, "Get on with your life, you've been grieving long enough" when the process appears to go on too long. This attitude toward another's pain can cause the bereaved to feel more desperate and alone.

Excessive grieving can be upsetting to watch, since most people feel helpless when faced with the grief of a friend. They avoid their friend because they don't know what to do.

Listening to the grieving person is always helpful. People need to talk about their pain in order to release it. We must spend time with our friends who are feeling the pain of grief. It's possible they don't have the strength to ask us to help them, so we should make our help easily available to them.

We are given a great opportunity to serve others by being there for them in their grief. Our friends who are mourning the loss of a loved one will show us the way to help. We need to be sensitive to their individual needs.

Certain friends may need us to sit quietly with them; others may need to cry or to be taken out to dinner. Don't be afraid to reach out. Your love and concern will be greatly cherished.

A deep reverent belief in the afterlife and in reincarnation are the strongest shields against excessive grief. Knowing that those close to us in spirit can be disrupted by our grieving thought patterns should prevent us from holding on to our grief for prolonged periods of time.

We all miss those we love and wish they could be on earth with us. We all find it difficult to say good-bye even when we know it's not forever.

The conviction that there's no death—only a change of form—will make it difficult to hold on to grief for long periods of time. It would be like sobbing uncontrollably because a friend was off on the vacation of a lifetime.

My gifts that have allowed me to see the other side and to receive messages from the departed have helped me and others to understand the process of passing on. These gifts have made me fearless in the face of death. But these special gifts don't protect me from feeling human emotions.

My life has been greatly enriched by many who've

passed on. The memory of their lives is never far from me. They've left the world a better place by their presence. I strive to live my life as a tribute to them. I handle the passing of friends as I would like mine to be handled. I cry because I miss them and then I let them go. It's a compliment to be missed, since it implies that we've affected the lives of others. But it would break my heart if anyone spent time and energy grieving my immortality.

The act of serving others is a great tonic for grief. We can't bring those we miss physically back to us, but we can serve their memory by helping others. Going on with our lives doesn't mean that we're disloyal to the departed. We can be faithful to the memory of those we love while we carry on with living.

Death is a temporary parting. We will be reunited with those we love. We must keep the memory of our loved ones alive through our passion for life. Each moment on the earth is an opportunity to help someone.

Miriam

Miriam lost her husband and went back to work one week later. Her friends all said that it was too soon, and criticized her for being disloyal to her husband's memory. Miriam wasn't bothered by the gossip. She received a message from her husband, Lou, in a dream.

"It was so real that when I woke up I thought Lou was in the room with me. He'd been gone for about twelve hours when I had this dream. He was covered in light and looked very happy. He'd been very sick before his passing and now he appeared to be in perfect health. He told me he'd come to help me because he'd felt my sorrow and tears. He let me know that it wasn't necessary to cry for him, that we'd be together again in the spirit world. He told me I must go on living to the fullest. He couldn't be happy knowing I was depressed."

This experience convinced Miriam that she could and should go on with life. She didn't worry about the opinion of her friends. Lou's happiness was utmost in her mind. Through this action Miriam, too, found peace of mind.

Let Us Not Live or Die with Regret

Steve passed over from cancer. When I saw him at the hospital he was in a state of rage, lamenting all the things he hadn't done that he'd meant to do.

"I worked twelve hours a day to have the money to do things. I was going to do them as soon as I had the time. My sons would ask me to go on trips, but I refused to take time off work. I was terrified that I'd miss a big stock trade and lose money. Why didn't someone stop me and tell me to live right now? I neglected my family because money and position were my goals. I have lots of money and no life left to spend it in."

He was grieving over the way he had lived.

Cindy

Cindy arrived for her appointment looking very depressed. Her father had passed over a year ago and her pain hadn't lessened. She sobbed as she spoke about his passing.

Cindy's dad had remarried shortly after his divorce

from Cindy's mom. Although it had been an amicable divorce, Cindy had never been able to forgive him for breaking up the marriage. Her father and stepmother did everything possible to show Cindy they loved her, but Cindy remained angry and resentful. She was rude to her dad and his new wife. When he was in the hospital dying, she refused to see him even though he kept asking for her. She now regretted her behavior and was consumed with guilt.

She was seeing a therapist three times a week, but her guilt persisted. Her behavior became self-destructive. She began to drink excessively and to miss work.

As I listened to Cindy I tried to stress to her the need for self-forgiveness. The last thing her father would want was for her to suffer for past mistakes. In his blissful state he understood Cindy's behavior. But it was hard to get through to her.

I was ready to give up, when I saw White Feather standing next to Cindy. He'd arrived to help. The astral screen came down in front of me and I saw Cindy's father. I described him to Cindy in detail.

There was a yellow kite above his head. He wanted me to tell Cindy that he loved her and was perfectly happy flying his yellow kite. He stressed that it would give him peace if she let go of the guilt. The picture faded and White Feather left.

Cindy was shocked. The yellow kite was one that she'd given her dad for Father's Day the year before her parents divorced. The day she and her dad spent flying the kite together was one of her happiest memories. This message confirmed that her father was fine and that he loved her. It helped start her on the road to self-forgiveness.

Cindy returned for a session a year later. With the support of therapy she'd been able to give up her self-hatred, and the depression was gone. She made peace with her stepmother, and even found that she liked the woman. Cindy had vowed she'd never make the mistake of waiting to tell people she loved them.

She still felt sadness over her past behavior, but the intense guilt had been replaced with understanding. She no longer felt the need to grieve for her past mistakes.

Many people live in a life-or-death struggle for material gain. The pursuit of money becomes so all-consuming that there's no time left for any spiritual life. We rush through life, always in a hurry, asking ourselves where the time has gone.

How many times have we heard the expression that someone worked himself to death? Think of my client Steve, who passed over from cancer. He'd spent his whole life acquiring wealth and power and never had a leisure moment to enjoy the fruits of his labor.

We must work in order to live, but we must try to think of balance. Our lives fly by because we're too busy to enjoy them. This is a major reason for the grief and regret many feel as they lay on their deathbeds. These people are grieving over the choices they made in their lives.

When we take a vacation, we have the time to move with greater leisure. When we're not overwhelmed by the needs of everyday existence, life seems much simpler. When we aren't in a state of chronic worry, we can have fun. We seem to savor our experiences and life regains some of its lost wonder.

We mustn't wait to appreciate all that life has to offer.

Clare

My friend Clare, who passed over from brain cancer, spoke from her deathbed. "I can't believe how much time I wasted by worrying about things that now seem unimportant. I was desperate for approval from people and constantly worried that I wasn't successful enough. I neglected my health because I wouldn't stop working long enough to get a checkup. I thought that money and position were the keys to being respected. Now, as I face death, I mourn my life."

Diana

Diana found out she had inoperable cancer. The doctors gave her six months to live. She took the news with great dignity and decided to spend what time she had left enjoying herself. Diana was a workaholic who'd always found it difficult to take a vacation. Only on hearing the news of her impending death did she start to enjoy her life, traveling to Europe with her sister and doing other things she'd never given herself the time to do: In retrospect she would've lived her life differently.

"I did nothing but work, putting in hours at the office and working at home at night. I must have been quite a bore: Work was all I talked about. Because of this, my life has passed by in a whirl. I never took time to have fun or to contemplate my spiritual beliefs. Now I deeply regret it. Please tell people that money and success are fine, but there's more to life. Don't wait until you're dying to start living."

* * *

It broke my heart to feel the pain these people experienced on their deathbeds. Their pain was a result of choices made while living. Work is an important part of our lives, but the passion for money and power leaves us with a terrible emptiness.

I had a conversation with Lawrence shortly after Diana's passing about the tragedy of missing out on life. This was what he had to say:

"The rage to accumulate wealth leaves man little free time for leisure. Modern man would learn a great deal from studying other civilizations. The ancient Athenians lived simple, frugal lives. They were satisfied with a lifestyle that now to us seems like poverty. A great deal of their time was spent outdoors. Their social life took place in nature. Athletic games and theatrical performances took place outside. Houses were used only for eating and sleeping. Little effort and less money were needed to keep them in order, as they didn't bother with fancy furniture. Think of the time and money modern man spends just furnishing and maintaining the home. The Athenians had fine exercise habits and ate in moderation. They enjoyed wine but not to excess. Their conversations took place in the fresh air, not around tables laden with food and drink. These habits led to long, healthy lives. Since their physical needs were simple, they required little money. That they loved literature and drama is evidenced by the great works left to us by such writers as Euripides, Aristophanes, and Sophocles. Their plays were produced for the enjoyment of the general public, not just a select few. Everyone took part in politics. This lifestyle allowed everybody a great deal of time to accumulate knowledge. It is sad that modern man uses most of his energy to make money to buy things that he doesn't need. A simpler life is a happier one."

I thought about my client Diana as I recalled Lawrence's words. Sadly, she learned very late in life that the acquisition of money wasn't the key to happiness. She'd spent most of her time earning money to buy things that are temporary. The simple things in life like a walk in the country, or a good conversation with a friend, aren't expensive. Unfortunately, most people don't appreciate this fact until they're in or near the spirit world.

Lawrence Helps a Grieving Mother

A client of mine lost her twelve-year-old daughter in a tragic accident. She died when the bike she was riding got hit by a car. Dozens of friends came to support the family in their grief. The loss of a child is one of the most painful events that can occur in anyone's life.

My client Martha was inconsolable. She needed love and support and she needed time. This wound went very deep, and there would be no quick method of grieving. Martha suffered from survivor guilt. She couldn't understand why she was alive and her daughter, Beatrice, was gone.

In her grief Martha lost her will to live. She felt hopeless and she didn't believe the pain would ever lessen. Her husband was very worried because he felt she was suicidal. He had his own grief to cope with, but he'd gone back to work and was also exercising to help re-

lease the anxiety. Martha couldn't force herself to do
anything except go to therapy once a week. Her husband
went with her, but the depth of her grief frightened him.

During this period of time once again I saw Lawrence. He was standing outside a card shop in the Village. Lost in my thoughts, at first I didn't see him, then
he cleared his throat. Looking up, I saw his smiling
face. We walked for a few blocks and then stopped for
lunch. We got settled and ordered soup and salad. I told
Lawrence about my concerns for Martha. As he listened
I could see he understood Martha's pain.

"This is a great test for your friend. It seems like an
impossible one. It's important to see her as often as you
can. People don't need to grieve alone. They must talk
to people about their feelings. Only time and knowledge
will help your friend to go forward. She believes in the
immortality of the spirit, but when she's faced with the
reality, her faith is shaken. What good are philosophies
if we can't lean on them during times of testing?

"True love isn't possessive. You create the body of
your child, not the soul. You don't possess your child.
You're allowed to watch over your children for a short
while and then they are in the hands of the lords of
karma.

"Martha isn't ready to let go. Not many people are
able to release their loved ones easily, as this takes a
very strong belief in the afterlife and complete selflessness. Your friend must find ways in which to serve others. This is the greatest tonic for grief. She must be
helped to help others. She is too overwhelmed to find
the way alone. You, my child, can lead her to an appro-
priate road of service. She's lost in her grief and we
must show her the tunnel that leads toward the light.

she's able to reach out to another in need
..... grief diminish. This isn't to criticize her need to
mourn.

"Didn't the great master say 'Blessed are they who
mourn, for they shall be comforted'?

"I would like to add, Blessed are they who serve, for
they will be served. Service is the way to comfort and
be comforted."

We parted outside of the restaurant. As I watched him
walk away, I thought about what he had said. I needed
to think of a way to help Martha start living. She was
so grief-stricken, she couldn't do it alone.

I was walking down my block toward home, when I
found the answer.

Sara, a young girl who lives in my neighborhood,
said hello to me. I looked at her and realized she was
the key to help Martha. She was a lovely thirteen-year-
old who'd lost her mother two years earlier. Everyone
in my neighborhood knew her and we all felt terrible
for her loss. Her father was a lovely man and he'd
given Sara the love and stability that helped her mourn
her mother's passing.

I told Sara about Martha. She listened with an understanding beyond her years and said that she'd love to
meet Martha. I was able to arrange a meeting.

It was difficult to get Martha to come with me to
Sara's. I was so vehement that Martha gave in to my re-
quest. I knew that what I was doing was risky. Martha
could have an adverse reaction to meeting this mother-
less child. But I remembered Lawrence's words: "You
must find a way for your friend to help someone," and
proceeded anyway.

I buzzed Sara's apartment, and she let us in. Martha

had no idea what I was doing. We entered and I introduced the two and told Martha about Sara's loss. Martha said nothing. Sara walked over to Martha and took her hand. It was as if she were the mother and Martha the child. She led Martha to the sofa and they sat down. She put her arms around Martha and told her that she was very sorry about her daughter's death.

Martha still said nothing. I began to worry that I'd done the wrong thing. Then ever so slowly Martha put her hand on Sara's head and started stroking her hair. Sara reacted by putting her head on Martha's lap. Martha then let go and sobbed. Sara kept repeating that everything would be all right. After a few minutes Martha dried her eyes and asked Sara how she felt. Sara talked about her own loss with Martha.

Lawrence had helped Martha through his great wisdom. She needed to be guided to a person who needed her. At first Sara was helping Martha, then they reversed roles. Martha's doing much better now. Sara and Martha have become great friends. They are missing their loved ones together.

Change

Death causes change for the departed and for those left behind. Change is difficult for most of us, but it can also make us strong. Nature doesn't allow us to stagnate. It presents opportunities for growth through change. Death is the ultimate change. It relocates us into a finer, more peaceful world.

We aren't always prepared for change, so when it happens, we're caught off guard. We mustn't become so content with our lives that we aren't able to adapt to change. We must accept the inevitability of change and embrace the opportunities that it presents us.

Paul

Paul lost his wife of thirty years. They'd been inseparable. After a lifetime of hard work he retired and was looking forward to traveling with his wife. Then just as all their plans were made, she became ill and passed over quickly. His total world was disrupted and he didn't know how to cope with the change.

Paul had never tried to make friends. He was not one to reach out to people. His wife provided all the companionship he needed. It had never dawned on Paul that his life could change. He was now presented with a difficult test.

He surprised everyone. His brother expected Paul to lie down and die with his beloved wife. He showed a different side of himself. He started living every day with passion. He joined different groups and clubs and started to make new friends. He took art classes and began painting, things he'd always wanted to do. He accepted his loss with dignity and went on living. He told me that he missed his wife. He thought about her every day. But he felt they'd see each other again. For now he was doing the best he could to accept and embrace the changes life had presented him.

Helen

Helen never recovered from the passing of her husband. It's been twelve years since he passed over and she still keeps his clothes in the closet and all his shaving items in the bathroom. Friends think it's a bit creepy to go to Helen's house. Despite all their attempts to help her move on, she remains locked into the past.

Excessive grieving over a long period of time can make the mind unbalanced. Still obsessed with her dead husband, Helen lives a haunted existence. She is haunted not by spirits but by memories of the past. She has become isolated and practically housebound. This is especially sad in a very vital person like Helen. Her inability to cope with change has stolen her happiness. It is nice to keep things that belonged to those we loved. Pictures of the departed and other mementos can be warm, comforting reminders of those who've gone on. But it is clear that Helen never learned that the greatest honor we can pay the departed is to go on with our lives.

Paul was able to accept the changes that his wife's passing presented. Helen buried herself with her husband. Her life is an example of the unhappiness we create for ourselves by living in the past. Change isn't always easy, but it can be life's way of opening new doors.

A Great Teacher Passes Over

On a Sunday morning my phone rang at six A.M. Lawrence's voice startled me. He informed me that he was sending the driver to pick me up in one hour. His voice had a serious tone I hadn't heard before. He went on to tell me that Sir William was dying and he had asked to see me.

"Lawrence, I'm so sorry. I'll be ready to leave in an hour."

Sir William's face flashed before me as I dressed. I remembered back to five years earlier when I was sitting with him in the city, listening to some of his musical compositions. There was a kind of holiness about this great man, and I always felt very happy in his presence. What he taught was quite simple.

"People suffer from heartbreak because they haven't learned to think properly. One's thoughts should be focused on compassion and understanding. The higher self that exists within each of us isn't controlled by personal desires. There is great nobility in learning to forget ourselves. The greatest life that man can live is one that is motivated by the desire to serve humanity."

I looked at the clock and realized an hour had passed. I hurried to the front of my building and saw the waiting car. We arrived at the house quickly.

Lawrence greeted me at the door. It was the first time I'd ever seen him looking tired. He had an unearthly calm about him and appeared to be in a semi-meditative state.

He explained that Sir William suffered from a blood problem that resulted from a past karmic situation. Although this would be his last incarnation with any physical problems, the current situation couldn't be avoided. He went on to tell me that he'd been with his teacher for the past seven days and knew the end was coming very soon.

"It is no longer necessary for him to inhabit his physical body. It is ready to be discarded. I will miss him being with me in the physical, but his spirit will be in contact after he has a period of rest. I'm very happy that his time for moving on to his real home is near at hand. I merely wish him to be as comfortable as possible as he passes over."

I remembered that Lawrence was a doctor. His fatigue was from caring for Sir William. He loved his teacher and wanted to serve him until his last moment on earth. These two great souls had been meditating together, so Lawrence appeared a bit unearthly. He told me to wait for a few minutes in the library and went to attend to his teacher.

I stood at the window in the library, looking at the majestic mountains surrounding Sir William's beautiful estate. The first time I'd visited this home, Lawrence and I experienced the beautiful mountain Deva (angel) together during a hike in the mountains. This angelic presence lives on top of the mountains, and is a force and feeling of beauty beyond description. Lawrence had told me to experience this beautiful deva by going into the silence. "If you look closely, you will be able to see this force. You will certainly be able to feel it if you allow yourself a moment of silence."

I moved away from the window, closed my eyes, and became one with the silence. I felt as if I were being held in the arms of the peaceful devic force once again. I felt an intense happiness and freedom. I opened my eyes and the library was filled with a golden light.

Lawrence came in and stood next to me for a moment. I took a deep breath and looked into his eyes. He seemed very tranquil and happy. "It's time to say goodbye." He led me to his teacher.

I entered the room in which Sir William was resting. He was breathing with difficulty, but this didn't affect his spirit.

"I have waited for you, my child, in order to say good-bye. Though we haven't met many times together in this life, I've known you in many previous ones."

He then told me some personal things he felt I needed to be aware of. He stressed that Lawrence would be there when I needed him. I mustn't worry about things in life that weren't important. All I had to do was my very best with whatever life presented to me.

He then told me to sit next to him for a while. He was too tired to continue talking. Lawrence entered the room and the three of us sat together in silence. The vibration in the room was calm and beautiful. At that moment I didn't feel like crying. Sir William seemed happy—as if he were ready to go on a wonderful trip. Lawrence was reverent and serene as he looked upon his dear teacher.

I then heard organ music faintly in the background. I knew it was coming from the other side. Lawrence looked at me and nodded. Sir William seemed to be asleep.

The words of the Master Jesus, "When two or more are gathered together in My name, there I am in the midst of them," passed clearly through my mind.

This was a very sacred event and I could see and feel visitors from the spirit world. A few more moments went by and Sir William breathed a deep sigh. He let go and went *home*.

Death is rebirth into the life of the spirit. Sir William would rest and then he would begin helping us from his side of life.

When I looked at Lawrence, I began to cry. These